MY FIGHT FOR
RECOVERY

MY FIGHT FOR RECOVERY

A Story of Overcoming Life-Threatening Brain Surgery

ROB PLASKAS

MY FIGHT FOR RECOVERY
A STORY OF OVERCOMING LIFE-THREATENING BRAIN SURGERY

iUniverse books may be ordered through booksellers or by contacting:

iUniverse
1663 Liberty Drive
Bloomington, IN 47403
www.iuniverse.com
844-349-9409

Because of the dynamic nature of the Internet, any web addresses or links contained in this book may have changed since publication and may no longer be valid. The views expressed in this work are solely those of the author and do not necessarily reflect the views of the publisher, and the publisher hereby disclaims any responsibility for them.

Any people depicted in stock imagery provided by Getty Images are models, and such images are being used for illustrative purposes only. Certain stock imagery © Getty Images.

ISBN: 978-1-5320-9511-5 (sc)
ISBN: 978-1-5320-9512-2 (e)

Library of Congress Control Number: 2020902873

Print information available on the last page.

iUniverse rev. date: 02/26/2020

CONTENTS

Don't give up. Don't ever give up.
—Former North Carolina State
basketball coach Jim Valvano

PREFACE

When I was in my late teens, I was a fairly popular seventeen-year-old high school student. I was funny, friendly, and handsome, or so I was told. I like to believe that was true, at least about the handsome part anyway. I was a decent athlete who started on my baseball team. Everything was fine, or at least as fine as it could have been for a guy in his late teens who, like everyone else at that age, was trying to come to terms with life as a young adult. I looked to the future with optimism, hope, and faith.

Then things went terribly wrong. I was diagnosed with a benign tumor in the left temporal lobe of my brain. To say I was scared would be the world's biggest understatement. The doctors said they'd keep an eye on the tumor and that if it decided to grow or play some other dirty trick, they'd have to saw a hole in my skull and yank the damned thing out. The only upside to the potential surgery, other than the obvious of not having a growth thriving in my brain, was the possibility that the procedure could also end my epileptic seizures.

Then the inevitable happened. The tumor grew.

"You have to have the surgery, Rob," my doctor said, his face grim. "You've got no other choice now. The tumor is likely to keep growing, and your symptoms will get worse. It'll be harder and harder for me to excise the tumor."

Oh great, I thought. *This is just what I need.*

I wasn't happy about having to undergo the operation, but my doctors said I had to do it. Or else. If I didn't have it done … well, let's just say the alternative wasn't the greatest. So, I had the surgery, and things went sideways. During the operation, I suffered a brain hemorrhage caused by a rupture in my internal carotid artery branch deep in my brain. The surgeon placed me in an induced coma as I lost massive amounts of blood. I essentially suffered a major stroke, leaving me with right-side paralysis, severe speech impairment, significant short-term memory loss, and lifelong dependence on anti-seizure medication, which mostly worked but not always.

Today, I am forty-two years old and work for the Illinois General Assembly as a communications analyst in Springfield, Illinois, where I earn an average income. I have lived in my city since 2004 and bought my house in 2007, in a nice neighborhood on the west side of town. I attend a huge Christian church and a religious support group, and I volunteer regularly by greeting people who come to our services, because I owe my life to Jesus. I have great friends who care about me and allowed me into their lives because I was always optimistic, funny, and caring. I love socializing, playing sports, traveling, wine tasting, exploring, eating chocolate, and smiling.

I am a brain injury survivor. And surviving quite well. Most brain hemorrhage survivors who are adults with similar circumstances to mine are not able to walk or talk without difficulty. Older adults with brain hemorrhages usually die within ten years because of many medical complications, or so says the data on stroke.org.

I wrote this book because I want people to know that survivors of a severe brain injury can accomplish many recovery goals if they have determination, willpower, and a positive outlook on their new lives, and if they are willing to do hard mental and physical work. They can develop skills to handle workloads of research and develop creative writing skills to finish a memoir, with the will to publish it. I have shared private details of my recovery because I want readers to understand brain injury survivors do not have to diminish themselves or their family relationships during their relearning and rehabilitation exercise activities.

My recovery shows how some survivors of severe brain injuries can recover and have productive lives if they work hard at their physical, speech, cognitive, and emotional therapies. They can accomplish some of their recovery goals if they have confidence, determination, and the willpower to succeed in their new lives.

During the past two decades, despite my injury, I have come to love my new life and friends who have given me support and encouragement throughout my long journey of recovery. I would not have, eventually, discovered the strength and willpower to keep going in my new life if it were not for the early support and encouragement I received during the first few years after my surgery. In time, I learned to embrace my injuries instead of hiding them, as I had done earlier in my recovery. I gained more confidence through my family, friends, and girlfriends and eventually developed a great attitude toward my new life.

I hope this book will inspire others who have either suffered serious brain injuries or are close to those who have. There is hope. There is quality life. It's not always easy getting there. The road to a better life can be long, arduous, and often frustrating, but my story is testament that the journey is worth pursuing. We all have our challenges. I believe the truest test is to overcome adversity with a positive attitude, even when you want to quit. Rising up to greet each new day with a sense of can-do and hopefulness is the essence of a peaceful and satisfying life, and getting to that point, even if life seems to have dealt you a barrelful of lemons, is what really matters.

CHAPTER 1

Brain Surgery

Wednesday, January 4, 1995, the day before my brain surgery, I got up refreshed in the morning and went to my high school. I did not have to go to school, but I wanted to say goodbye to all of my close friends before I left for the medical center. I was slightly nervous and scared that day because I knew it was possible things could go very wrong during surgery. The person coming out might be different from the one going in. I was worried I might not see my family and friends again, as they knew me, if I had complications in my surgery.

As I was leaving at noon, the weight of the upcoming surgery pushed me down emotionally and spiritually. I fought against depression as I said goodbye to more of my close friends. I found myself wandering around the halls of my school, yearning for normalcy to return to my life. I made my way to the weight room, a place where I felt at home. No one was there. The lights were dim. The room smelled of old sweat and cleaning solutions. I did a light set of exercises to remind myself I would be back in a few weeks or a couple of months, when I was done healing from my surgery. As I was leaving, I looked back at all the equipment I had used to get myself in excellent shape for my surgery. I had exercised more, doing a daily routine, after I was diagnosed for the second time with my benign tumor. I would be back in the weight room once I got back on my feet again, after my recovery from surgery. At least that was what I told myself on that momentous day.

I had no idea that I was about to face traumatic and life-changing events well beyond my control. It was as if I were a crimson leaf floating on a swift river in autumn, the current sweeping me downstream, along with the other leaves, in a change of seasons as inevitable as the passage of time, the incoming or outgoing tide, the path of the moon as it traverses the night sky. Some things, like death, are facts of living. As a teen, facing what would, and often does, scare most adults, I proceeded into the operating room (OR) with the stupidity of youth, the endless hopefulness of a kid who thought he was invincible, thinking that the little tumor growing in my head was like a zit to be popped, cleaned out, and salved.

Oh boy. Was I ever wrong. Looking back on it now, I'm glad I didn't overthink the situation. It was bad enough as it was, and it would've been worse if I had known then what I know now.

When I was leaving my high school, before I got into my car, a snazzy 1992 tan Ford Probe I had begged my mother to buy for me, I stood there looking at it, fighting back the tears. It occurred to me that I might never see my school or my friends again if something went terribly wrong with my surgery. I looked back for a moment at my school to remind myself of all the cherished moments I'd had with my friends, classmates, and teachers.

I recalled my sophomore homecoming dance and going out to a nice restaurant with friends, near Elburn, Illinois. After the dance, some of us went to a friend's house, where we continued to party and have fun. That was my first time drinking alcohol. I can only smile at the silliness of my early years, the innocence, and the limitless possibilities that seemed to linger just over the far horizon.

I sighed, fought back tears, and got into my car. I wiped the tears away, looked around, and was pleased that none of my friends were nearby, close enough to see me crying like a baby. The enormity of what was about to happen cloaked me in its awful weight. I realized that this could be the last time I saw my high school. I realized that my life as I knew it could be over forever. The stark reality of that made me want to throw up. My hands trembled as I gripped the steering wheel.

What other choice do I have? I thought. "You're gonna do this," I said aloud. "You've got to go through with it."

I fired up the engine and began driving aimlessly through town.

I cruised past the house of my close friend Scott, slowed, and stopped in front to cherish all the moments we'd had together. I had met him in school my freshman year, and we hung out a lot. We would talk, often about women, go on adventures, and sometimes play pranks on other friends. There was this one time, on a weekend, when I was hanging with Scott and we bumped into another kid from our class.

The kid was pissed because we both liked the same girl. He was about to get physical, but Scott stepped in and told him to back off. I always appreciated him for that.

I passed by a few more of my closest friends' houses to remember all the times of joy I'd had during my childhood and teenage years. I passed most of my old girlfriends' houses, where I had parked to kiss them inside my car and outside by the front door of their homes. I followed up by driving past my elementary and middle schools to remind myself how much I had learned in my life.

And then I drove home. My mood darkened further when I walked into the house and saw the despair and fear in the eyes of both of my parents, even though they tried valiantly to hide how they felt. Their hearts were heavy with the stress of not knowing what to expect with such a potentially problematic surgery, which was scheduled for the following morning. They were afraid something could go wrong in my brain because my benign tumor was close to my hippocampus region, and they had good reason to be afraid.

We had to drive a distance to the medical center in Chicago, Illinois, far enough that we needed to book hotel rooms for the evening. I distinctly recall a funereal aspect to our final departure from a home that none of us knew would ever be the same again. We only had the sneaking suspicion that significant change was on the way.

When we reached the hotel, we checked in. Dinner in the hotel restaurant was awkward. We watched a little TV after we ate, but I could tell that none of us were paying much attention. I certainly wasn't. My brother tried to take my mind off the surgery with his jokes, and I was grateful for that.

"I think it's time for some shut-eye," Dad said, hitting the button on the remote to turn off the TV.

Mom looked like she was about to cry. Then she made a brave face. I could almost see her willing herself to smile. She got up from the sofa as I stood up from the loveseat.

"Darling," she said, giving me a hug. "Everything's gonna be okay. You know that, don't you?"

I said I did, even though I didn't believe it. I don't know how I knew it, but I somehow knew that this night would be the last one of its kind going forward. I gave my mom a hug and said, "I hope you're right."

Then my brother and I went to our hotel room and tried to sleep. I did a lot of thinking about my neurological problems. My brother talked to me all night long about silly things. We talked about lifting weights. He made fun of me, saying I didn't lift very much, even though I could lift more than he could. We talked about my new relationship with my girlfriend, Tracy. We talked so much I did not even get to sleep.

In the early morning, I got out of bed and took a long shower. Suddenly I was very nervous about my surgery. I imagined what might happen if I did not make it through surgery and my family's reaction when my neurosurgeon told them I passed away. I thought back to one of the first meetings with him. He'd told me I was in good hands and that he had not lost a patient yet. I'd felt a lot better after that.

My surgery was scheduled for 5:00 a.m., so my family and I walked to the Center at four in the morning to get ready for my operation and to get settled down. I was reckless when I crossed the street to enter the Center because I was not looking for traffic. The Center had a busy street in front of its entrance, so I needed to walk across the road carefully, but I walked across the street carelessly. My mind was on the events about to happen, and I was not focused on where I was walking. My parents got very upset with me for crossing the street the way I did. I was lucky the streets were not too busy at that time. They already had to worry about my surgery. Had I gotten into an accident outside of the Center, it would have crushed them. They were very nervous that I might not see them again, alive, after my surgery because of the increased growth of my benign tumor a month and a half ago and the risks that accompanied the procedure.

When I checked in at the surgery desk, I was more nervous than I had ever been. It clicked in my mind I might not live, but I knew my neurosurgeon was going to do his best to save my life. I could not concentrate on anything except my surgery and praying to God I would be fine.

My family did not get the chance to say much to me in our waiting room because an energetic nurse came quickly to pick me up. I was told to sit in the handicapped wheelchair so she could push me to the intensive care unit (ICU) upstairs. Being pushed in a handicapped chair was a bit disturbing to me because I did not have full control of my body. My nurse had a confident look on her face, so I felt somewhat calm, considering the circumstances. I was leaving my family, who had been with me since day one of my lesion and benign tumor diagnosis. I said goodbye and that I would see them in a few minutes in the ICU.

My nurse pushed me into an elevator and pressed a secret passcode on the keyboard to go to the ICU. When I got there, I changed into surgery clothes and went into the bathroom to urinate. When I was done, I pulled down a metal chain next to the toilet to flush, but I pulled the wrong one. Instead, the chain set off an alarm the whole room could hear. The nurses looked at me like I'd had a heart attack. I said I was fine and lay down on a gurney, then waited to be rolled into the operation room (OR).

My family came into the ICU soon after to soothe me by standing on the right side of my gurney. I felt secure seeing them, even though it was only for a few minutes. I felt my mother squeezing my hand hard. I squeezed back, less hard. She did not say anything to me because she was nervous and scared. She did not know if I would survive my surgery. She could barely keep from sobbing.

She was compelled to baptize me because I had not been baptized before in my life. All she could think of was the passage from Isaiah in the Bible, 43:1–2, "Do not fear for I have redeemed you by name. You are mine. When you pass through the waters, I will be with you; and when you pass through rivers, they will not sweep over you." She spoke the words and with her finger used her tears to make the sign of the cross on my forehead. I said she did not need to baptize me because my surgery would be a success. A few seconds later, I felt a warm tear fall onto my right cheek, and I almost lost it.

I was trying to be calm, but my heart was beating faster than it ever had. I thought I was going to have a heart attack when I was about to leave for surgery. I again reminded myself my neurosurgeon would make my surgery successful because he had not lost one of his patients. As the neurosurgery team assistant was pushing me out of the ICU, I said goodbye to my family one last time.

Unless you've been in a similar situation, you'll never be able to understand the emotional gravity of such a moment, but I'm sure you can imagine it. The health-care system sucks all control from your life. In some ways, it's worse than the disease itself. That feeling of helplessness, the fact that you have to put all your faith, your entire life, for that matter, into the hands of strangers is enough to make a person want to walk away from treatments altogether. Yet, most of us, even at the height of our frustration, toe the line and do what we're told by the guys and gals in white lab coats and green or blue scrubs.

It took a long time to get to my surgery room even though it was on the same floor. As they wheeled me down the long corridor, I could see the right wall was made entirely of windows. I wanted to see my family one more time and give them my great smile so they would know everything would be okay. I wanted to give them a big hug one more time, but it was too late. I was wheeled through double doors into the surgery room, where a beautiful young nurse with a great smile was waiting for me by the surgery table. I flirted with her for a minute and asked if she would go out on a date with me after my surgery. She smiled and laughed because she was much older than me.

A few minutes later, my neurologist came into the surgery room.

"How you feeling, Rob?" he asked.

"Just peachy," I said, wanting to leap up from the table and run screaming from the Center.

"That's what I like to hear," he said, shooting me a fake smile.

As we exchanged inane small talk, one of my neurosurgery team assistants began putting needles inside my body, which were attached to the blood I had given earlier. If something went wrong and my brain bled immensely, those needles would save my life. They would give me blood reserves that would flow fast into my body so I would not die of blood loss. My arms and legs were strapped down to my surgery table. I was so focused that the restraints really didn't bother me. They put a white sheet on me and pulled it up to my chin. This helped keep me warm in the cold meat locker of the OR. My neurosurgeon shaved my head bald so he could draw a line with a marker to guide his cutting saw. My cut line went symmetrically down the top of my head, slightly to the left, and made a loop right behind my left earlobe. He fitted my head into a metal device so I could not move for my craniotomy. It was surprisingly comfortable. My craniotomy was the surgical removal of part of my bone from my skull to uncover my brain. Specific tools would be used to remove a portion of my skull called the bone flap. The bone flap would be briefly removed, then returned after surgery.

I was kept awake during surgery because it reduced the risk of damaging critical brain areas that control speech and other skills. The worst part of being awake during surgery was the feeling of the Novocain needle my neurosurgeon inserted in my skull many times. The needle was painful, but I dealt with it because I only had to do this once in my life. I also knew it was nothing compared to what was coming. I was pleasantly surprised when he finished with the Novocain needle. I had no sensation of my skull being open. After my skull was open and the outer layer of my brain was carefully cut, my neurosurgeon began my long surgery.

I felt no pain when my neurosurgeon began cutting and suctioning my brain tissue because the brain does not feel pain. If my benign tumor was where my seizures occurred, it could be near the parts of my brain that controlled vision, movement, and speech. He asked me questions and monitored the activity in my brain as I responded.

He avoided parts of my brain that were involved with my functional areas. My responses helped my neurosurgeon to ensure he treated me in the correct area of my brain. I was hoping I would not lose my whole memory, but even more worrisome, I knew what was at stake. My life.

My neurosurgeon found my benign tumor and began removing it. He was almost done with no complications in my surgery, but he was stunned as his suction tool was going into my hippocampus region, which has a key role in my learning and memory. Based on his review of my magnetic resonance imaging (MRI), he had not anticipated having to get that close to my hippocampus. My neurosurgeon was very cautious when he started to remove the last part of my tumor because it was in a significant portion of my hippocampus region. Sadly, the tumor had played another dirty trick. It had grown, and it had decided to go where no tumor should go.

Suddenly, I became aware of a spike in tension in the OR. I don't recall everything that was said, only that it turned out that my inner brain began bleeding immensely because of a ruptured, internal carotid artery branch when he removed the last piece of my tumor. My vessel wall was too weak to hold my blood back. I heard him ask the nurse for a clamp, but I did not panic. I was nervous, but I did not show it. I did not ask questions because my neurosurgeon would get distracted when he needed to concentrate on my brain. Somehow he was able to stop the bleeding with his big fingers and put three metal clamps on my injured vessel. He took minutes to get them in the right position.

During that time, he told me to raise my right forearm when they took off my right arm restraints, and I did so. I was almost panicking inside when he said that. I decided to move my right fingers just in case, without him saying so.

I was in normal condition while this was happening. I did not know that in less than one minute I could die. Because it took so long to stop the bleeding, my neurosurgeon decided to knock me out with medicine. I heard him tell his anesthesiologist, "Medicine." When he said that, it meant nothing to me. I was about to not be able to breathe on my own because of blood loss and oxygen. I was getting oxygen by a breathing apparatus through a tube that was inserted in my mouth and down my throat.

My neurosurgery team used extraordinary measures to get my vital signs back to normal levels, by getting blood back in my body as fast as they could. I suffered a hemorrhagic bleed in and around the brain. The damage wreaked on me would be determined by the size of the brain hemorrhage, the amount of swelling in my skull, and how quickly my bleeding was controlled. I lost about a liter and a half of blood in the process of my surgery, according to my neurosurgeon. Just to put that in perspective, an average adult weighing between 150 and 180 pounds has between 4.7 to 5.5 liters of blood, or between 1.2 and 1.5 gallons. Losing 1.5 liters out 4.7 is a lot. Too much, as it turned out.

My neurosurgery team gave all their best efforts to keep me alive. My head was packed in ice to slow my body function down, and I was put into a temporary barbiturate-induced coma.

I later learned my coma was used to protect my brain during my severe brain bleed, and it reduced the metabolic rate of my brain tissue as well as my brain blood flow. With these reductions, my blood vessels in my brain narrowed, decreasing the amount of swelling in my brain. When my brain swelling was reduced, the pressure on it decreased. Later on, one of the neurologists at the Center would tell my family that the coma gave my brain time to circulate blood through my smaller blood vessels in the area of the initial flow of blood.

I had suffered the equivalent of a massive stroke and came very close to death because the flow of blood in my brain disrupted my normal circulation. My bleeding raised the pressure inside my skull to dangerous levels. My neurosurgery team put me on an intravenous line (IV), so I received nutrients in my body to give me strength to help me recover.

If I survived, there was a good chance I would have grand mal seizures caused by electrical snafus in the brain. These are really nasty events that trigger uncontrollable muscle contractions and loss of consciousness. The seizures could be controlled by anti-seizure medicine if an intelligent neurologist could find the right ones. If no one could find the right meds, I could have spells because of the vessel blockage and disturbed blood flow.

I remember two dreams I had in the coma. In one dream, I was in a surgery room by myself with interior windows all around me. I was dumbfounded, lying down on the operation table. A few nurses were outside of the windows, not watching me. I wanted someone to see me so I could be sure my brain surgery was successful. I thought my family and doctors had abandoned me. The panic I felt is difficult to describe even now. When you face a serious, possibly terminal disease, everything changes. You suddenly realize that even with all the love and support in the world, you're still pretty much alone.

In the second dream, I was in a small, white, brick room by myself with no windows. I was getting off the operation table to stand up, wondering where everybody was. I felt I was alone, with no support or encouragement to get through this horrifying moment in my life.

CHAPTER 2

The Diagnosis

In July 1994, after my sophomore year at Oswego High School in Oswego, Illinois, I was playing basketball in our summer league at my school when I suffered a very exhausting, simple partial seizure, called a spell. My spell was a result of my epileptic activity localized in the left temporal lobe in my brain. My consciousness was not impaired, and I remembered what happened during and right after my spell.

I was playing defense as the opposing point guard came up the court. I was in my stance to defend him, and a strong spell happened, accompanied by a unique aroma that took my breath away, turned my face pale, and made me feel as though blood was going from my arms down to my legs. The odor reeked ... like burning tires. I later learned that this distinct smell is a classic sign of something gone terribly wrong in the brain.

The spell lasted about a minute. I have had these kinds of spells before, but this one was stronger. I was drained and had a tough time walking off the court to sit down on my team's bench to rest and recuperate. After talking to me, my summer league basketball coach decided not to put me back in the game.

"I don't like the sound of what you're saying, Rob. This could be serious."

"I don't feel so good," I said.

"You look terrible. Sit the game out, okay?" the coach said.

I was so scared and nervous about my spell I didn't even know who won that game. It could have been the spell that caused me to forget the score. After the basketball game, the varsity basketball coach told my father something seemed very wrong with me. The varsity coach often spoke with my summer coach when he had problems with players. The varsity coach said I was having trouble remembering the plays other players could easily remember.

Due to my history of epilepsy, my mother decided to take me to the local emergency room to get an MRI that day. I was worried the entire trip there that this spell had caused something terrible and that my diagnosis would change for the worse. I learned by watching documentaries that some epilepsy patients had to have brain surgery. I did not wish to have brain surgery to cure what I was afraid would be my new diagnosis. I feared the severe consequence of death if something went wrong on the operating table. Of course, I would have surgery if I needed it to save my life. Until research finds other cures, surgery remains one of the best hopes for epilepsy patients to have a lasting result.

The ER doctors, after looking at my MRI, saw what could have been a benign tumor. They believed it could be what had made me experience my big spell, but my pediatric neurologist at the hospital near Chicago, Illinois, would make that decision.

Soon after visiting the ER, we went to my pediatric neurologist. I had already been diagnosed at the hospital with a brain lesion and scar five years earlier, in 1989, from an MRI. A brain lesion is an area of injury or disease within the brain. Understanding brain lesions can be complicated. That's because there are many types of brain lesions. They can range from small to large, from few to many, from relatively harmless to life-threatening. There can also be many causes of brain lesions. After this MRI in 1989, due to my diagnosis, I went back for an MRI every three months for a two-year period.

I was diagnosed with epilepsy as a freshman, in 1993. The difference between this spell now and my old spells were the symptoms and how hard on me they were physically and emotionally. If not treated quickly, I could have this unusual aroma every time I had a spell, for the rest of my life. I wanted to be healthier and live a peaceful life without the anti-seizure medicines I had been on for almost two years. My mind was racing.

My brain lesion was downgraded in 1991 from a lesion to just a scar by the hospital's pediatric neurosurgeon. Although my previous medical records revealed a lesion on the left temporal lobe, he was focusing on my right temporal lobe. I believe the hospital's radiologist who took my MRI and my pediatric neurosurgeon who examined it made that mistake because I had metal braces on my teeth at the time. My metal braces interfered with the MRI, and the two doctors could not find my brain lesion. It was difficult tuning into my brain. The MRI tuning process is similar to tuning a radio to a precise frequency or radio station. My tuning process was complicated because of the metal in my mouth.

My benign tumor in my brain was rare. There are two types of tumors. A benign tumor is an abnormal growth of cells that serves no purpose. It is not a malignant tumor, which is cancer. It does not invade nearby tissue or spread to other parts of my body the way cancer could. In most cases, the outlook with my benign tumor was good. It could be severe if my benign tumor presses on vital structures such as my blood vessels and nerves. Therefore, sometimes they require treatment.

Now, in July 1994, the MRI taken at the ER of the local hospital had revealed a left temporal lobe abnormal mass in the same place as my previous tests years ago. It was more extensive and significant. I felt my stomach drop as the doctor gave me the bad news.

Damn. I don't want to have brain surgery! I thought.

My lesion, now suspected to be a benign tumor, was located deep in my left temporal lobe. By 1994, my braces had been removed, which is one reason I believe the doctors from the local hospital were able to properly diagnose me. I was crushed and deeply depressed because, according to the hospital's pediatric neurosurgeon in '91, my lesion had gone away or was dormant. Years later, after my surgery, I researched to see if he still worked at the hospital. He did not.

My pediatric neurologist at the hospital in '94 explained that my benign tumor was close to my vital brain areas and arteries. I knew when he told me I would have to have the surgery. After speaking with him, because of the seriousness of the diagnosis, my mother decided to take me to a different hospital for a second opinion. At a medical center inside Chicago, the neurologist found mistakes in my treatment from the hospital's pediatric neurosurgeon years earlier. He advised I should go back and see my doctors from the hospital and get an MRI scan from their department. He would review the new MRI to be sure there wasn't a mistake made at the ER at the local hospital. I had not had an MRI at the hospital since I was released from my pediatric neurosurgeon at the hospital in July 1991 ... not since he made the big mistake of looking at the wrong side of my brain.

I believe the neurologist from the Center notified my doctors at the hospital after reviewing my MRI scans I had done at the local hospital, from 1989 through 1991. I was worried about my dangerous new diagnosis. I was concerned about my parents because they had gone through hell to do all the right and cautious things for my medical care. I was depressed and had panic attacks for a couple of days when I was alone in my bed and car. I was not sure I would live much more because of serious complications that could arise in surgery. I kept thinking, *Why me and not someone else who had this benign tumor!*

My doctors from the hospital wanted me to go to their Neurology Department immediately to do an examination to find out if the Center neurologist was right. I was given another MRI so he and his faculty could compare it to my previous MRI from the ER at the local hospital.

When my middle-aged, pediatric neurologist from the hospital came into his meeting room to see my parents and me, he wore dress pants and a nice shirt with a beautiful tie, covered by his white coat to make him look professional. He told us my benign tumor or lesion was new, and it was not my old lesion. He added that I needed to have brain surgery now. If I decided to have my pediatric neurosurgeon at the hospital perform my surgery, he would not be able to remove my entire benign tumor. They both believed it was too close to my important motor regions.

When he told my parents and me the terrible news, we were speechless as we faced the full gravity of the situation. *Help me God.* I stared at him and wanted to punch him in his face because I had the possibility of dying if I did not have brain surgery very soon. I did not raise my voice to tell him what I thought of his facility's error regarding my new diagnosis, even though I wanted to. I wanted to scream, to blame someone, but I knew that would not make my tumor disappear. My mind was racing on what to do next. I needed to ease my nerves in my serious condition. Once we left, I did not think he was professional because his facility had misdiagnosed my tumor.

My family and I were stunned because my benign tumor was in the same spot as my lesion was five years earlier, in 1989, in the local hospital's MRI. It had grown from the size of a pea to the size of a walnut. I had an MRI done on January 3, 1990, and the radiologist at the hospital thought my lesion was just a growing scar, which was wrong. Years later, after my surgery, I again researched to see if the radiologist still worked at the hospital. He did not. My walnut-sized tumor was extremely dangerous, and I needed an excellent neurosurgeon to remove it.

Before any neurosurgical decisions, my parents wanted another opinion from other neurologists and neurosurgeons.

They wanted a correct diagnosis of my tumor. My parents decided to go to Mayo Clinic located in Rochester, Minnesota. They heard it was the best in the country to get a medical diagnosis. Mayo's neurosurgery and neurology departments were ranked number one in the country.

My parents quickly took all my medical records and MRIs we could get from the hospital and the local hospitals to a brilliant neurosurgeon and neurologist at Mayo on July 18, 1994. We wanted accurate evaluations of my benign tumor. We also needed to know the risk of surgery with a much larger tumor.

Going to Mayo was very stressful on us because we had to wait two days before a neurologist and neurosurgeon could see us. The next morning, we traveled from our house in Illinois to Mayo, which was about five hours away. My parents decided to get our minds off worrying about our meeting the next day. We went to a bookstore to buy books and magazines to keep our minds less stressed because there was a lot of tension about my condition.

When we had our meeting with the neurosurgeon and neurologist, they studied all of my medical reports and MRIs. Much to our dismay, they said that the new diagnosis from my pediatric neurologist at the hospital was correct. When they saw my MRI from when I had my braces on my teeth years ago, they saw my lesion immediately. I thought to myself, *Why couldn't they have been my doctors back then? Why couldn't the doctors I had have seen what these doctors saw? Even if my braces had caused some interference, these doctors didn't let it stop them.* I was mortified. They felt steps had been overlooked by my doctors when I was released in 1991.

The young neurosurgeon at Mayo was confident he

could get my entire tumor removed because a large part was due to a cyst. Brain cysts are not brain tumors, because they do not arise from the brain tissue itself. Although they tend to be benign (noncancerous), they are sometimes found in parts of the brain that control vital functions. A cyst does not cause any symptoms, and the majority of them do not need to be treated at all.

I believed the neurosurgeon at Mayo did not have enough experience in brain surgery. Today, he is the chair of neurosurgery at Mayo. I would compare him to a national basketball league all-star and most valuable player of neurosurgery. My parents felt Mayo was a considerable distance from our home, and if I had complications in my surgery, it would be a difficult drive if I needed to stay for prolonged recovery time. We decided to stay close to our home and try to find a great neurosurgeon there so I could have my whole family with me.

Northern Illinois had distinguished medical centers and hospitals with top-of-the-line neurologists and neurosurgeons for us to find the one that fit my needs. My parents sought them out to find the right one for my serious condition. First, my parents decided to make an appointment with a well-known neurologist, because many doctors informed them he was the best in the country at studying brain tumors. His accomplishments and achievements in his neurological career spoke very highly of his rank and reputation.

My parents and I went to the neurologist's hospital in a northern suburb of Chicago so we could consult with him to be sure my tumor required surgery. He carefully explained what he saw in my previous MRIs. He listened to what we were told during the consultations we'd had with the hospital, the Center, and Mayo doctors. He explained I would need surgery. He advised me to get another MRI to compare my tumor to my last MRI, to determine the rate at which it was growing. He explained the necessity of having the new MRI done in the same plane of section as the last MRIs were done over the past years. He wanted to gauge my tumor's growth.

My parents and I were impressed by the neurologist's knowledge of tumors and lesions and his concern about the rate of growth. He explained my situation on levels I could clearly understand. He was especially careful when explaining to me the risks, and I found him to be someone I could trust. Of all the neurosurgeons, he spoke highly of the top, skilled neurosurgeon from the Center, who I made an appointment to consult with. This coincided with our wish to be close to home.

My parents and I thought the Center would be less stressful for our family to travel to and from for my surgery because it was a comfortable ride (about an hour) from our house. It would be easy to visit after my brain testing and surgery, especially if any complications arose. Plus, I would need as much support and encouragement in my recovery afterward as I could get. I gave my medical case to the Center because I believed in the neurologist.

Today, the Center is ranked as one of the best hospitals in the country in neurosurgery and one of the best for teaching pre-medicine students and treating patients. The Center had all the right medical support I needed. The elderly Caucasian neurologist who recommended I have my surgery at the Center assured us my neurosurgeon had an outstanding record for being successful at brain surgery operations.

In late July, my mother and I had a meeting with my new

elderly neurosurgeon in his large office. The windows were along one wall, and a long table in the center with a desk ran perpendicular at the end of the room. He welcomed us with a handshake before we sat down across from him at his expensive desk. He had nice glasses, so I thought he was intelligent.

He went over his surgery procedure and how he would remove my tumor. I would have a left temporal lobectomy surgery done. Temporal lobectomy is a four-hour surgical procedure targeting removal of the anterior three to four centimeters of the temporal lobe. This area of the brain lies just behind the eye and above the ear. He told me I would be awake during this process because my benign tumor was close to many of my motor skills. He believed there was a 90 percent chance of no complications if I had my surgery very soon.

I could tell the Center's neurosurgeon would not be nervous when he was under pressure because of his knowledge, experience, and stature. I believed he was the right man to do my surgery because he cared about me and wanted me to succeed in my life. After asking me personal questions to get to know me, he said things like "Don't worry, Rob. We will get you taken care of and playing sports again in no time." He was one of the best neurosurgeons in the country. As important, I felt comfortable around him.

My parents agreed with my neurosurgeon and wanted to do my surgery immediately. My assigned young neurologist said he did not believe my benign tumor required an urgent surgery. However, he did tell me I had six months to get my tumor removed or there was a higher risk of complications. Also, there was a massive line of patients ahead of me waiting for surgery by my neurosurgeon. He was excellent at his job. My new neurologist at the Center scheduled me to have surgery on January 12, 1995. Later, I was scheduled for January 5 because of my parents' persistence and unrelenting advocacy.

After my surgery was set, I saw my neurologist from the hospital on August 5, 1994, for the last time in my life. He did his examination on me and strongly recommended I have brain surgery as soon as possible, because my tumor was growing. By that time, I was not in shock because all of my doctors had already said I needed surgery.

My mother had a final meeting with the hospital's pediatric neurologist, without me present, a month or two later. She said she had honest medical conversations with brilliant doctors who told her my true diagnosis. My mother was not happy with his treatment of me. She believed he and his hospital were irresponsible for having missed careful reviews of my MRIs before and after my braces were on. He walked out of the meeting without any further words.

Looking back on that period of my life, from my vantage point of today, I realize now that the going would only get tougher. Fortunately for me, I didn't let the full reality of the ordeal I was about to face really sink in. In retrospect, it would not have been possible for me to know in advance just how risky my surgery would be. Intellectually, you can understand when a doctor says, "Hey, we'll do the best we can, but I can give you no guarantees." But on an emotional level, you can only understand when you've actually experienced something similar yourself. For me, it was almost as if I was watching myself in some sort of TV show, a reality show, of course.

Ultimately, I think my upbringing helped me get through

it all, both before and after the surgery. Growing up as a child, I idolized my brother, Aaron, and liked what he liked when it came to sports activities, such as baseball, and fashion styles, like rolling our pant legs into cuffs. The only thing we disagreed about was our tastes in music. He loved heavy metal, and I loved rock. I tried to learn from his mistakes and hid things I did growing up so I would appear to be a perfect son to my parents.

In elementary school, I was a bully to classmates who did not play sports and were weak physically. Then, when I was in second grade, I was the one getting bullied. When that happened, I knew how my classmates felt when I had picked on them. I felt scared and intimidated by the bully because he was stronger than I was.

My speech ability back then was poor compared to my peers. My whole life, I struggled with pronouncing the letter R. I could not correctly say my own name, which often came out as Wobby, nor could I properly pronounce any R words. It wasn't exactly a stutter, but even with the help of a speech therapist, I could not use R properly. Because of this problem, a couple of Aaron's friends picked on me. They called me names, like Wob. I stopped using any R words when speaking. Verbal bullying caused me to be ashamed of myself because I could not say one letter.

When I was in seventh grade, I had a scare in my English class because, every day, my teacher called on a student to read a portion of a book out loud. I was hoping he would not call on me. If he did, I would admit I could not say r's correctly. I was too popular to admit I had a speech problem. By some miracle, he did not call on me the whole year.

In academics, I was excellent at math. It was my favorite subject, and I was put into an advanced math class with the elite students every year until high school. I did not have many questions about homework or studying because it came quickly to me. I knew I was going to be someone in my professional career, later in my life, because of my determination and hard work when studying.

I began liking girls a lot in middle school. When I was in sixth grade, I really liked a cute blonde girl in my class named Christina. We met one afternoon at the end of our English class, when school began in the fall. I got to know her throughout the school year. She was caring and intelligent. She lived by me, and we would walk together to school in the mornings. I did not ask her to kiss me because my parents would giggle if they found out I had a girlfriend. I hated being embarrassed. I did not stand up to them because I was afraid they might laugh at me.

In my free time with my friends, we would go on adventures to mysterious places. We would get into trouble, as kids often do. One adventure was hanging toilet paper on telephone wires above a highway close to downtown in Oswego late at night. Drivers were dumbfounded when they saw what we did. We were laughing behind a bush because we had committed a little crime and gotten away with it.

I was building my popularity among my friends and classmates. I hung out with two groups of friends in my class, and I had a great time with both. One group consisted of athletes and preps, and they did what their parents wanted them to do. We did party, but most of the time, we behaved like most teenagers. The second group were athletes and wild friends. They went on real adventures. We drank alcohol and partied when we got the chance. If our parents found out about our immoral actions, we would be in big trouble. I knew I would be grounded.

One time in the summer, when I was sixteen, a group of us went to Starved Rock National Forest to chill and smoke marijuana at the great rock. Starved Rock is named after an event that started with the stabbing of Chief Pontiac of the Ottawa tribe, who was attending a tribe council meeting in the 1760s. He was stabbed by another tribe member. The chief's followers started a great battle between the two tribes. The opposing tribe took refuge on the great rock. The remaining followers of that tribe died of starvation, giving this historic park its name, Starved Rock.

My whole life, I played sports. I began playing soccer in my youth, but I got sick of it because I stood around too much and found it boring. Instead, I played football because I liked hitting opposing players. I was okay at basketball, but I kept acting like I was the best point guard around when I was not. Baseball was the sport I flourished in, and I was one of the best in my class. I had talent, leadership, and the will to succeed. (It didn't hurt that my father was a high school Hall of Fame baseball coach at West Aurora High School, after he took his team downstate four consecutive years in the 1970s.)

I was excelling faster than other players. I got so mad at myself when I had a bad game, either pitching or batting, because I knew I could do better. Throughout my Pony League and high school experience, my batting average was around .375. If you do not know baseball, a .375 average is good. When I was a sophomore, I had big intentions. I was hoping I could get an athletic scholarship to a college, as my father did, so he would be impressed.

My father, who later became a legendary baseball coach, was a great wrestler in high school and college. He won the Big Ten Championship his junior year when he wrestled at

Northwestern University. I tried to wrestle, but I got pinned all the time by both excellent and bad wrestlers and wasn't very good.

I worked out every day in high school to improve my sports skills and be in the best shape I could. I did all kinds of weightlifting and cardio techniques to build as much muscle and be as toned as I could in every area of my body. I wanted to be an elite athlete and dominate in any sport I tried. I bonded with more athletes in the gym because we loved to get in shape. On the side, I wanted girls to give me a double take to boost my confidence and self-esteem.

All of those ambitions seemed to be within my grasp prior to the emergence of stronger symptoms that indicated my spells might be getting worse and that they might be something more than just spells. Looking back, I can honestly say those were some of the best days of my life. They were certainly not carefree. As I've said, I faced all the same troubles that commonly go with adolescence. Yet, compared to the rabbit hole I was about to go down, those worries seem trivial now.

What's that expression again? You don't know what you've got till it's gone.

CHAPTER 3

Misdiagnosis

My first diagnosis of a lesion in my brain was in the spring of 1989 when I was eleven years old. I had lied to my parents about a headache from a hit to my head with a hockey stick. I was playing hockey in my neighbor's garage with Aaron and other friends on a Sunday. When I got home, I told my parents about the hit to my head. I informed them I had a headache when, in fact, I did not. I told them this because I didn't want to go to school on Monday. When Monday came, I told my mother my head still hurt and I needed to stay home and rest again. I was lazy and wanted to skip school.

My mother took great care of me and, because she was worried, decided I needed to see my pediatrician to get an examination as soon as possible. I had an appointment the next week because my pediatrician was booked with patients. She examined me and said everything appeared normal, physically and mentally. Because it had been a while since my hockey accident, she ordered an MRI of my brain at our local hospital, to make sure nothing had happened.

I was excited about having an MRI because I had never before been examined for anything abnormal in my life. The only thing I did not like about the MRI was the injection of dye used to light up my brain. I hate needles going in me because they hurt. After my MRI, as I was leaving the room, my radiologist gave me a big smile. I believed everything was okay. I was confident while waiting for my pediatrician to come into the conference room, back at her office, to get my results.

When my pediatrician came, she said I had an unknown mass in my left temporal lobe in my brain. She spoke with no emotion at all. The temporal lobe processes memories, integrating them with sensations of taste, sound, sight, and touch. She referred me to a great pediatric neurosurgeon at a hospital near Chicago, Illinois.

I was dumbfounded, stunned, nervous, and scared because I did not understand what was going on. I had always asked my parents questions, and they would answer them, but now they could not. I was afraid of seeing the pediatric neurosurgeon because I knew it was possible the unidentified mass could be diagnosed as something terrible. I believed my parents might be upset at me because I had done something terrible to myself and failed to tell them about any number of incidents from my past. I liked to play rough. I'd suffered head injuries before ... quite a few of them. And now it seemed like the beast had come home to bite.

When my family and I had a meeting with the pediatric

neurosurgeon in March 1989, he looked at my MRI and studied the report on the unknown mass. He diagnosed me with a lesion and scar from an old injury, which was the size of a pea. There were signs of calcification near my lesion, indicating it had been present for years. A calcification happens when calcium builds up in the brain's tissue. This buildup hardens and disrupts the brain's normal processes. His diagnosis was not a death threat, but he needed to track any growth. If it was growing, I would need surgery immediately.

I started to collapse when the doctor was almost done explaining his diagnosis. His nurse caught me in time, saving me from more injuries. A wave of nausea swept over me as the doctor's words became garbled in my head. I clutched my stomach, fought hard not to vomit, and lost the strength to stand. Slowly I began to sag. As I said, I was only eleven. It seemed like the world had just ended.

"What's going to happen to me?" I asked. "Am I gonna die?"

The doctor said no, it wasn't likely that I'd die, and that it wasn't even a certainty that I'd need surgery at all. Yet, deep down, I knew I was headed for the doom and gloom. At the moment, nothing seemed right, and everything seemed wrong. I could see that my parents were about to freak out as well. That didn't help. It scares a kid when they see parents about to lose it.

The doctor and I talked about my head injuries before my hockey accident a month before. He needed to find out what caused my abnormal mass and how long ago it happened. My parents and I told him how I once fell off my changing table as an infant. I crashed into a fence at the age of seven and dropped out of the homemade go-cart that my grandfather helped me build, then hit the ground with my head. I might have had concussions somewhere along the line because of any number of falls and blows in sports activities. The biggest accident I could recall was when I was about six years old. I fell out of my tree house and landed on my head. When I got up from the ground, I was dizzy with some pain. My uncle Joe, who was watching me at the time, saw it happen and came running over. He was thankful I wasn't paralyzed.

The doctor wanted to determine the nature of my abnormal mass before he considered surgery. Was it growing? Was it shrinking? Was it causing any unusual sensations such as the smell of burned rubber? Seizures? He arranged for me to go to the hospital for an MRI and an appointment with him every three months for about two years. A few months later, my mother told the doctor about medical books she read saying metal braces on your teeth interfered with MRI imaging, and he agreed. She postponed getting me braces, which I was told I needed in order to straighten my teeth. In 1990, with my persistence, she decided I should get braces, but she asked the doctor if it was okay. He said yes because, after monitoring my abnormal mass for several months, it had not grown.

I hoped my abnormal mass would not grow ever. I already had so many goals I wanted to achieve in my life. One of my goals was to be successful in a profession later in life. I wanted my parents to be proud of me for studying hard and making a difference in other people's lives.

During the following several years, I would live my life one day at a time. Life was short, especially with the threat of having surgery. If something were to go wrong in surgery, I was worried about my parents. They and I were nervous and scared about my abnormal mass from then on. It's difficult to describe what that was like. It was almost as if I'd acquired a dark companion, a force that lurked just below my consciousness all the time. And then, of course, it would pop to the surface of my thoughts and sit there grinning at me, taunting me, making me believe that my life was over when it really wasn't. I found myself having to rebuke the dark companion to get him to go away, but he never did. He never has, not even to this day. I've just learned to live, knowing that my situation is what it is and that railing against things you can't control just makes things even worse.

In July 1991, the doctor from the hospital said my abnormal mass appeared to be shrinking, based on my MRI. He believed it was no longer a threat to me. I was released from his care with instructions to notify him if any changes occurred, such as strange aromas. I believed him when he told me it was no longer something to worry about. Obviously, my response was natural. What prisoner on death row would reject the commutation by the governor?

I was excited with the hospital's doctor's new diagnosis because I believed I could have a normal life again as a young teenager. I was confused though, because I did not think my abnormal mass would entirely shrink in size. Anyway, I once again had enthusiasm for school and playing sports without the fear of having surgery. I was free from fearing that I would die ahead of my friends. I was liberated from my dark companion, or so I thought.

My parents were happy and laughed with joy because it was a relief of intense pressure for them. Even the hospital's doctor shared in their happiness. My parents and I felt free after dealing with two years of frequent MRIs and visits to the hospital. As I left, the hospital's pediatric neurosurgeon was still studying my MRI.

A few years later, when I was about fourteen, when I did not have anything to do, I often played basketball at my house, alone. One time, I had a spell with a strange feeling that lasted about a minute. It was like a smell of mucus and swallowing my tongue's saliva. I felt a significant blood flow that began in my shoulders and slowly went down my arms and legs. I had a blank stare and was smacking my lips. I could not handle people talking to me because I needed to concentrate on what I was doing at those times. When my spell was over, I was tired for a few minutes. I did not tell anyone about my spell yet because I was too proud to admit I had a problem with being very tired. I was not playing for very long. I couldn't admit to people what I was thinking, that I was slow and out of shape.

My spells could be related to cells around my unusual mass that had developed abnormally. It could be due to an imbalance of chemicals in my brain caused by my unusual mass. Together, it could interfere with the normal electrical activity in my brain.

A few weeks went by, and my spells kept occurring while I was playing basketball. I finally told my mother about it, and she notified the hospital's pediatric neurosurgeon. He suspected I had epilepsy and referred me to a first-rate pediatric neurologist at the hospital on May 13, 1993, when I was fifteen years old.

I was excited to meet the doctor because I believed he was a well-known and superior pediatric neurologist. I believed he would know what was going on in my brain to cause my spells. I was confident he would take care of me and my recent diagnosis of epilepsy by the hospital's pediatric neurosurgeon.

After my doctor did his examination of me, he agreed with my pediatric neurosurgeon's diagnosis. I had an epilepsy disorder, which was not life-threatening. My epilepsy or seizure disorder was a medical condition that produces spells affecting a variety of my mental and physical functions. A spell is when a brief, strong surge of electrical activity affects part of my brain. I did not have convulsions and loss of consciousness, but my spells lasted about a minute. I was relieved because my epilepsy was manageable without surgery. My doctor started treating me with anti-convulsion (anti-seizure) medicines for the next year and a half.

I was somewhat concerned my friends and classmates would look at me differently because I had epilepsy. They might think I could have seizures at any time and be worried I could die. They might think I was weak and less confident playing sports, so, with the exception of a few close friends, I never told them about my diagnosis. If one of my friends did not think I was a full athlete because of my epilepsy, I proved them wrong by going out, working hard, doing my best, and excelling at baseball.

My anti-seizure medicines worked well for a few months, but then my spells returned. I returned to my doctor, who put me on a different medication. I never really saw the spells as a big problem because I was always glad it wasn't the alternative of having brain surgery. I counted myself lucky I was not having seizures worse than my spells, which are known as grand mal seizures. If I had a grand mal seizure, it might cause me to lose consciousness and violent muscle contractions.

My mother and I met with my new neurologist at the Center several times during the fall of 1994. He was all business and usually quite rushed in his patient office. He was not emotional when he laid out all the tests I needed before my surgery. I did not worry much about my surgery coming up in January. I felt confident everything had been arranged: place, date, time, and one of the best neurosurgery teams in the country. I bragged about my new doctors because of their career status at the respected Center. I told my close friends I would have my surgery after the fall semester ended and made sure they did not have to worry about me.

I did not know my parents felt anxious, unable to sleep, afraid, weak, sick to their stomachs, and very nervous about my serious condition. It was a heavy-hearted experience for them thinking about my surgery in January. Every day, they struggled with the feeling I was fighting against my surgery by putting sports ahead of my life. They wished I would have the surgery immediately. They thought the sooner I would agree, the better, because I would have a greater chance for recovery.

I desperately wanted to play football with my team, which I did. In retrospect, it was really stupid to play football knowing I had a tumor on the left side of my brain. I'm surprised my parents and doctors didn't forbid me to play. In any case, I was a moron and resisted any talk of moving my surgery up to September instead of early January. I wanted to see if my football team would win the state championship game. My brother's team won the state championship in 1992, and I was jealous. I wanted to be exactly like him because of his athletic ability and popularity among his teammates, friends, and coaches. I realize now that I was operating from a foundation of deep insecurity. My speech problems didn't help. Trying to live up to my brother, or to my grandiose image of him, didn't help either. So, I tried to make myself look like the big man on campus by excelling at sports.

My father told his coworker and friend, the varsity football head coach, about my surgery in January. My coach said I should have my surgery before the football season was to begin because it was a life-saving situation. He would have me as an inspirational leader when I was done recovering.

Instead of taking advice from my coach and my parents, I played football so I could help our team win another state championship. Our high school had one of the best football programs in the state of Illinois. We could go to the state championship game because we had excellent players that year.

My teammate and friend Mike was a High School All-American as an offensive lineman. A second teammate and friend, Joey, was the greatest athlete in our high school history because of his great ability to block, tackle, and provide leadership. He went on to the National Football League, where he played fullback for several seasons.

I believed our team would be undefeated that season because no team could match our strength and speed. I had great pride because our class had not lost a game yet in high school. I felt our team would coast through the playoffs and win the state championship for the second time in our high school's history. We made it all the way to the playoffs, but to my surprise, our team lost in the second round.

At the same time, in the fall, my relationships with female students blossomed. Every girl I talked to or flirted with was touched and hopeful they could become my new friend or I might ask them out on a date, or at least that's how I pictured it in my head. My best friends were girls. I loved them because they loved me back as a family member. They were popular, and I felt secure and more confident with them by my side.

I began dating in the fall and treated female students with respect and dignity. One brunette, skinny girl stood out in December. I liked Tracy because she was caring, intelligent, motivated, athletic, and very beautiful. We dated for a month, and I thought about her all the time as we grew closer.

One time, at the end of our date, when I was dropping her off at her house, I told her I was going to have surgery next month before saying how I felt about her. Before she got out of the car, I opened up to Tracy and told her, if there was a significant accident during my surgery and I was severely hurt, she should date someone else and forget about me. I believed we had started a real relationship, and I knew I would fall in love with her in the near future.

I was hoping for a big hug and words of support and encouragement for me to recover as soon as possible. My hope was dashed. She was silent when I was done speaking. I felt she was scared about my surgery and how dangerous my operation would be.

I had my last MRI in early November at the Center to see if my benign tumor was still the same size as it was in the early fall. To my surprise, it had grown a little in size. My mother and I were worried, so we had our last meeting with another of the neurologists at the same medical center. He wanted me to have surgery now because of my benign tumor growth. It was closer to my hippocampus region now, deep in my brain. Instead of listening to his recommendation, I waited for a month. I was scared of my surgery now, and my parents did not urge me, I thought. Finally, I agreed with the neurologist. My mother was determined to get my surgery date earlier than expected when she found out about my decision. My surgery was moved to January 5 from January 12.

I went twice to the Center to give two pints of blood in the ICU. These would be used for my surgery, in case of emergency. I was fine giving blood because it was not painful. They used a baby needle, and a nurse inserted it in my vein on my arm. When I was done, they gave me great orange juice to drink to help my body produce more blood. I had about a liter or two of orange juice each time.

On December 28, 1994, my neurosurgery team had me undergo a pre-surgery test called a cerebral angiography procedure. They had to find out if my benign tumor was touching any of my vital brain blood vessels. When I had the procedure, my radiologist inserted a catheter into my groin artery. While it was painful, I was able to deal with it. Using the catheter, he injected a special dye into my blood vessel that led to my brain. He took x-ray images, which showed blood vessel abnormalities in my brain.

He had me lie down on an x-ray table with my head held still by strong tapes on my forehead to prevent me from moving. My eyes and pupils were the only thing I could move. I had great peripheral vision, so I could see the surgery team working to get the test over with. He gave me a mild sedative to help me relax before my test started. I would not get nervous and shake when he put the catheter into the main artery in my groin.

Prior to the procedure, I was nervous the catheter would be very painful, but I had to do it. When the time came, I wanted my surgery to be successful in removing all of my tumor. I did not know how long the test would be until the tube was about to be inserted in me. My neurologist, who was at the procedure, said it would take about ten minutes and I would feel pressure and moderate pain. I was sad, but my life was at stake, so I tried to stay positive.

The catheter was then inserted in my groin artery and guided in through my stomach area, chest, and neck into my brain. Suddenly I was freaking out with the catheter going through my body and into my brain. I could have a stroke or some kind of complication. I reminded myself I had one of the best surgical teams in the country. Still, when you're in the middle of a procedure like that, it's tough to keep your cool. You feel utterly helpless, and you are. The loss of control is one of the worst aspects of being shoved into the medical system. You're at the mercy of other people, most of whom are too busy to really care about the person behind the disease.

My radiologist did the guiding by using x-rays taken of my upper body to move it to the exact positions to get to my brain. When the catheter got to my brain, he put dye through it and took x-ray images to see how the dye moved through my arteries and blood vessels. The dye helped to focus on any blockages in my blood flow. After the x-rays were taken of my brain, he removed the catheter from my body. My first-day procedure was done and had not been too painful.

My radiologist put pressure on my groin where the insertion was made. He waited for about fifteen minutes to make sure my bleeding stopped. He put a tight bandage on my incision and told me I needed to keep my leg straight for eight hours. If I did not keep my leg straight, I could have internal bleeding. My neurologist said my radiologist needed to do the procedure on both sides of my groin. My radiologist did the second procedure the next day because one side needed to heal.

On the first night, after eight hours of holding my leg straight, my mother and I were allowed to leave the hospital. We went out for dinner to a nearby famous pizza restaurant I had been looking forward to. We talked about my surgery tests and recovery once my surgery was finished. I tried to make sure my mother did not worry about me because I had faith my neurosurgery team would be successful, with no complications. I was expecting the same pain from the cerebral angiography procedure on the second day. I was happy with this test so far because I could bear it.

When I began the second test, that did not happen. My pain was unbearable during the whole procedure.

It felt like I was getting tortured for a long time. I wanted my radiologist to kill me, but I knew my family would be devastated not seeing me alive again. To make my testing time go by faster, I kept counting to one hundred, many times, so my pain would not be as consuming as it was. My determination and willpower helped me get through the procedure. I passed all of my tests and was ready and very confident for my upcoming surgery.

My mother was in the Center's chapel and then in my recovery room, alone, as my procedure was being done. She was not allowed in the surgery room. She prayed for me to be okay because she thought about how painful and frightening my insertion must have felt. She was proud of me for having endured so much pain and without complaining. My mother wished she could have taken on the burden of my procedure because she was older and could deal with my pre-surgery tests. She didn't want to see her son go through these trials. She told me all this much, much later. Yet, even then, I knew for sure that both my parents and my brother were stressed out about what was happening to me.

A week before my surgery, Mike, one of my cousins, called my parents and asked them if he could help take my mind off my surgery. Back in 1995, Mike was a newspaper, sports journalist in Colorado and was traveling with the Colorado Rockies franchise in Major League Baseball. He wanted to have a popular ballplayer help support and encourage me before I had to go into surgery.

Mike told Joe Girardi about my critical situation. Joe was an all-star catcher for the Rockies and later was a manager for the New York Yankees. At first, Mike felt a little uncomfortable asking Joe for a favor because it compromised his position as a journalist. He was supposed to cover ballplayers, not ask for favors, but he and Joe had a little different relationship. They would talk about baseball and their families all the time before games. Joe was the type of guy who did things for children and teenagers all the time. He believed the most important thing we should do is help others out.

I was in my room at home, sleeping, when Joe called me. He told me I was in great hands at the Center because they were one of the top hospitals in the country. He invited me to see him play at Wrigley Field, where the Chicago Cubs play, in the upcoming season so that I could shake his hand in person. When we were done talking and I hung up the telephone, I felt awesome! I would get to be in the presence of an all-star player when spring came around. He was praying for me, and the sincerity of his words touched me and gave me hope. I was ready for my surgery.

CHAPTER 4

Aftermath

Looking back on the day of my surgery and near death, I can't imagine what my family went through, even though they told me later about what happened when they got the news that my surgery had gone terribly wrong. They were all gathered in the private guest room, waiting for hours and hours for news. Suddenly, the phone rang. My mother rushed to answer it. My neurologist told her there had been a massive bleed in my brain, and extraordinary measures were being taken to save my life. He would come down to say more after my neurosurgical team had done everything possible to keep me alive. I know my mom was speechless for a few seconds before she said to my dad, "Rob's in trouble."

She relayed what the neurologist said with tears

streaming down her face. She fell into my dad's arms and just sobbed. "I'm so scared," she said. "I'm so scared for Rob."

"I know," Dad said. "We all are. We just have to have faith that Jesus won't call him home." He had tears streaming down his face as well.

I still can't fathom how much my father was struggling at that moment, because he is a very emotional person. My brother was stretching by taking a walk around the hallways when the phone call came. When he found out, he was crushed. He could not believe his brother was in critical condition. My family decided to go to the chapel to pray for my survival. Hours went by, and my family was still waiting for more updates on my serious condition. Finally my neurologist went to their waiting room to explain what had happened in detail.

He told them about how my neurosurgeon had almost finished removing my benign tumor without any complications when my hemorrhaging occurred. In spite of the burst of blood filling my open skull, my neurosurgeon immediately found and pinched the tear in my vessel, applied surgical clamps to permanently close my torn artery, and started intravenous blood to replace my loss of blood. It would allow time for my blood to pass through the vessels from my right brain to my left brain, where the massive hemorrhage occurred. He suctioned off the mass of blood filling my open skull.

My neurologist thought, from the size of my vessel, it was one of my internal carotid artery branches that gave way and caused my massive bleed. The carotid arteries are the two main arteries that supply blood to the brain. I had lost so much blood they'd had to use a mechanical device to keep me breathing. Some members of my neurosurgery team did not know if I could survive. As my neurologist talked to my family, he seemed shaken by the whole situation, according to my mother.

My mother was shocked and desperate over my neurologist's grim news. She was hoping for the best news about my surgery. She was nervous about when and if I would wake up because my heart rate could go up too fast, and breathing could be difficult. She was worried I could not speak or would have severe memory damage.

When I was stabilized, both my neurologist and neurosurgeon went to my family's private waiting room, at different times, much later in the day. They explained, in detail, what had happened during my surgery. They could not give any insight to my family at that moment, saying my recovery would be somewhere between the best or worst possible outcomes. They believed I would live because I was young and in great shape. Their direct and precise surgical explanation of my surgery and hope for my likely outcome helped my parents reach a bit of stability. They were still in a suspended state of shock that felt both unreal and frightening.

My family had to wait a few more hours to visit me because of the severity of my condition. My neurosurgery team had to attach a lot of medical equipment to my body so that they could monitor my brain waves and heart after my surgery. They did all of this, plus much more, so they could save my life. When I was settled, my neurologist went to the waiting room to let my family know they could come to see me in the ICU, but with my critical condition, they had to be quiet and could stay only a few minutes.

My family was overwhelmed, frightened, and almost breathless when they saw me. My head was 50 percent bigger than usual because of the swelling in my brain and the bandages used to wrap my head. I looked weak and fragile because of my massive loss of blood. They wanted to help me, but they could do nothing to save my life besides pray. Their memory of my critical state was locked in their minds forever.

My family stayed the night at the same hotel as the night before. They felt anxious and overcome with fear, and none of them spoke. They just sat there lost in their thoughts because they were all heartbroken. When my parents went to bed, they did not sleep at all because they wanted to see me as soon as possible.

Friday, the first full day after my surgery, my family hurried back from their hotel to the Center. They were too early to see me right away. They stood outside while my father smoked. My father was the leader of our family, and when he decided to go outside, my mother and my brother followed. When they returned to the ICU, they were allowed to see me. There was even greater swelling in my brain. Otherwise, there was no change in my status. My family was allowed to sit with me briefly and quietly in ICU every three hours, because my neurological team was very cautious about my status. They could not hold my hand or physically touch me because I could begin to wake up from the coma. All they could do was pray for me to heal and be normal again.

After the first morning visit, my brother went home because he wanted to grieve by himself. Some of my family and close friends came to the Center in the late morning. They were not allowed into the ICU but tried to give comfort to my parents. Everyone meant well, but my parents were very solemn and inconsolable. Later that day, my brother called Tom, one of my closest friends, to ask if he wanted to come along to the Center to see me. Tom said he wanted to go because he was my great friend from school.

On Saturday, the second full day after my surgery, my brother and Tom arrived. Only immediate family members were able to come into the ICU for short periods, but Tom was able to be there for a short time, thanks to my brother's influence with the doctors. My parents were sitting next to me when Tom came.

Tom was initially timid, but my mother hugged him and welcomed him to sit quietly next to me. He spoke softly to me and prayed I would wake up with no damage. My mother noticed my head turned slightly to my left, where Tom was seated, but I was deep in my coma.

Later that morning, during one of my family's visiting periods, they noticed a printed card taped to the top of my bed. My mother was overwhelmed because it was the passage from Isaiah, the same passage my mother had used to baptize me immediately before my surgery. Seeing those emotional words helped her to develop hope, emotional strength, physical endurance, and faith over the following decades of my recovery. She had stayed close to me all day during the permitted times. She whispered the words from the passage of Isaiah to me a few times as she was leaving the ICU, but I showed no response.

My neurologist encouraged my father to think about returning to work on Monday, to shift some of his focus and possibly lower his anxiety. After discussing it and being assured by my neurologist and ICU staff that they would notify him if there were any changes in my condition, my parents decided my father would drive home later in the afternoon, while my mother would stay at the Center through the night. It was difficult for my father to be so close to me and not be able to do anything to help. My neurologist arranged for a private room in the intern's dorm for my mother to get some sleep. She emphasized her wish to be immediately notified if my condition changed.

My mother's feelings were torn because she needed to be near me as much as possible, but my father needed her too. She would stay with me through Sunday evening, and if my condition was stable, she would return to our home for the night. That night, my mother felt alone and helpless in her dorm room because she could not be by my side to console me. In the short, restless sleep she got, she dreamed I was in the hands of God and an angel would protect me from any more injuries.

Sunday, the third day after surgery, my father drove to the Center in the morning to be with my mother. They talked to my neurologist about any extra risk involved if I woke from my coma suddenly. He seemed to think I would be all right if I did wake up. The whole day, I was still in the same state, with no movement. At the end of the day, my mother wanted to be with my father, and as she could not be in the ICU with me, she decided to go home to sleep.

Monday, the fourth day after surgery, my father returned to work with a broken heart. My mother returned to the Center, after the morning rush hour, to spend time with me, as much as possible. Finally, after four days, she could reach out and touch my hand. She could touch her baby boy. I could be touched because I had rested enough from my surgery and it was okay if I woke up from my coma, according to my neurologist.

My mother asked him what she should do to help me while I was still in the coma. My neurologist suspected I had a massive stroke because of my severe injury and I would be paralyzed on my right-side extremities. He explained and demonstrated what she needed to do to exercise my right foot during her allowed times. She should put on my basketball shoes to prevent foot drop. Foot drop is a sign of an underlying neurological and muscular problem. The foot drags on the ground when walking because it is difficult to lift the front part (forefoot). This unusual foot stride could cause me to slap my foot down onto the floor with each step.

My mother went to my bedside many times that day and did what my neurologist said to do to improve my potential right-sided paralysis. She put my basketball shoes on many times. She softly talked to me so she could give me hope if I was able to hear and understand her. I was not responsive. I would be her sole focus, now and for many months, if I woke up and lived. Her mind released some of her fears about the future as she concentrated on me one day at a time. Before my mother left the Center, she again requested a phone call from the ICU nurses if I had any changes in my condition. She went home late in the day to be with my father so they could support each other.

When my mother got home, she received a call of sympathy from her side of the family out in New Jersey. While my mother was speaking with them, she had another sense of me resting in God's hands, which were protecting me. She continued to recall images of God's hands that night and realized the images of me were to help her stay strong. Of course, I had no idea how she, my dad, and my brother were feeling during this time. For me, it was all nothingness, a blank sheet, except for the still-lingering presence of an idea that I'd visited a place few living people get to go. Later, of course, my mom and I talked a lot about that terrible time.

Monday night, my mother was sitting next to our home telephone throughout the early morning, but the ICU nurses did not call. She called the ICU around four in the morning to check on my status. My nurse had good news. When she rotated my body to my right side, which was done regularly, so I would not get bed sores, my hospital gown fell open, leaving my rear exposed. She saw me reach around to find my gown to cover up my behind with my left arm. She said I still looked and acted like I was in the coma. That behavior signaled my capacity for conscious thought.

To my mother, the news about my action was a sign of my self-awareness and I might be coming out of my coma. She had concerns that it might be too sudden. Nevertheless, she rejoiced that I had demonstrated my first conscious act since my medical crisis. When she came to visit me that Tuesday morning, she felt overwhelmed with more hope.

My mother went home again that night to be with my father. He was having a hard time being alone with his feelings for me. She talked to the ICU nurses about communicating regularly about my status by telephone during some more critical nights. She spent the night sitting in an old rocking chair in our living room, next to the phone, all night and the early morning, waiting for a status report. The nurses did not call, and she was worried with anxiety.

Mom told me later that the strain had almost been too much for her. I know I didn't cause my illness, but I still feel a little guilty sometimes when I think about how much pain I caused because I got sick. It's a fact that the afflicted person almost always feels responsible for the pain his or her loved ones feel when everyone is plunged into the murky pool of health care, treatments, diagnoses and prognoses, and the relentless march of the disease itself as it strives to consume everything you ever hoped for, ever wanted, and ever would be. It's important for anyone who's in the same boat as I was to understand that you didn't cause your sickness. And it's not your fault that, because you got sick, the people who love you felt sad, scared, angry, helpless, and even hopeless at times. That, sadly, is the nature of the beast when you get sucked into the world of hospitals and self-important doctors in their white coats.

Wednesday morning, the sixth day, my nurse called my mother around seven o'clock with good news. She said my neurologist had been in to check on me earlier, and he could not find his stethoscope. He asked her where it was. Before she could answer, I raised my left arm to point to a shelf above my bed where the stethoscope was. I showed signs of consciousness because I was seeing and hearing them and understanding what they were saying. I was aware of the location of the stethoscope!

Later that morning, what got my attention was my neurosurgeon's intern. He was taking the metal staples out of my skull. Each time a staple came out, it was even more painful than the one before. I was very relieved when the last staple came out, but the removal seemed like it took at least an hour, when in reality it only took a few minutes. While I was vaguely aware of what was happening, I was not fully awake yet. It usually takes days to fully come out of a drug-induced coma.

When my mother arrived at the Center, after the morning rush hour traffic, she was overwhelmed to hear I had awareness of the stethoscope. My mother still saw me as being in a coma because I did not respond to her, but she was optimistic about my ability to be able to understand when I woke up. She knew, for certain, I would be in God's hands from that day forward.

On Thursday, I was moved into a private intensive care room because my temperature was dropping to near normal. My temperature had been high, in the low hundreds, earlier in my coma. When a relative called my private hospital room telephone, I picked it up in the late morning. I could not talk, but picking up the receiver was a sign I was headed in the right direction.

My mother experienced two powerful feelings. Her heart was full of gratitude that I had survived my surgery, but it was also heavy with worry about the unknown quality of life I would have. She vowed never to give up helping me believe in myself and getting me the therapy and services I needed.

My mother studied, to learn about the nature of my brain damage, at the Center's library when I was in my coma, using as many resources as she could get. While none of the doctors could be certain about the extent of the damage that occurred during the surgery, they all said I wouldn't wake up unscathed. Damage had definitely been done. They just didn't know how much. She found the best independent therapists for my needs over the upcoming years. She began a long process of growing more hope and strength for our family and me. She focused on her determination to work toward our mutual family recovery, emotionally, through many therapies for many, many years. While I slept in that netherworld of a drug-induced coma, my mom girded for a battle that would go on for decades. Indeed, as I've said, I'm still recovering more than twenty-five years later.

CHAPTER 5

Awakening

I lurched awake, almost as if someone had thrown a bucket of ice water over my head. One second I was out, and then I wasn't. My eyes opened wide, and the bright lights of the hospital room almost blinded me. My heart rate soared as the panic set in.

Where am I? What the hell happened? Was I in a car wreck?

Then the stark horror of my new reality set in.

No, silly. You're in the Center. Some dude just sawed off half your skull, stuck some knives and other shit inside your brain, and yanked out a nasty walnut that was totally messing you up big-time.

Oh yeah. That's right!

And almost in the same thought, I realized I couldn't move the right side of my body. More panic. Outright terror, in fact.

Oh no! I can't move! Oh my God!

For most of us, such a moment would be unimaginable. And I hope for your sake it remains so. For me, it was real. Too terribly real. The warnings from the doctors poured into my mind like a reservoir that breached its dam. The voices all merged together into a babble worthy of Babylon. I thought I was going to go nuts in those first few minutes of my awakening. If I could've, I think I might have chosen to go back into my dark, deep sleep … back to the coma where nothing could hurt me ever again.

My massive stroke caused the paralysis. My right-side paralysis was one of the most common disabilities resulting from a stroke. As many as nine out of ten stroke survivors have some degree of paralysis immediately following a stroke, according to stroke.org. I was crushed, and I wanted answers right away because I feared I was disabled for life.

No one was in my room, so I tried to yell for help, but I could not make a sound because I had global aphasia. Global aphasia is the most severe form of aphasia. You can produce no recognizable words, have short-term memory loss, and can understand little spoken language. Usually, you can neither read nor write. It is possible to have fully preserved intellectual and cognitive capabilities unrelated to language and speech.

My global aphasia was caused by injuries to the multiple language-processing areas of my brain. These brain areas were particularly crucial for understanding spoken language, accessing vocabulary, using grammar, and producing words and sentences. My symptoms rapidly improved in the first few months after my stroke, but it was a lasting result of my injury. I still struggle to understand what people say to me. It takes work. And it takes a lot of patience and willpower on my part not to get so frustrated that I want to throw lamps out glass windows, or kick the dog, or whatever.

I hoped my injury was a temporary condition and would go away within minutes. I wanted to leave the Center to go home as quickly as possible. Usually, I do not wish to be stuck at home, but this was very different. I was scared about my state of mind, nervous and frightened beyond belief as I waited for my neurologist to come into my room to give my diagnosis.

I had to call my nurse or doctor to find out what happened to me and get water immediately because I was so thirsty. I was immensely dehydrated from my coma because of my loss of water intake. When I got water, I drank it fast and wanted more and more. My nurse gave me a bucket of ice so that I could suck the cubes all day long.

When my neurologist and my parents came into my room from the hallway, soon after my nurse, they did not say much to me and had blank looks. I pointed to my mouth, because I could not say what happened or I loved them. I pointed at my right arm and leg because I could not move them.

My mother came up to my bed to hold my right forearm, but I could not feel her touch. My panic increased. I pictured myself living life from a wheelchair, not being able to talk, not being able to even go to the bathroom without help, and I just wanted to cry. I wondered what I'd done to piss God off so much that he decided to deal me such a crappy hand from a deck of cards full of promise for seemingly everyone else but me. I know now that these thoughts are normal for a person in my position, but at the time, the despair and anger I felt was about as intense as any emotion I'd yet experienced, or have experienced since then.

She said, "Hey," softly, but no other words came out. She and I knew we were going to hear about my horrible diagnosis. They were not yet depressed, seeing me in terrible shape, but those feelings would come later in my recovery. They did feel an intense weight of anxiety because they felt they might lose me still. They wanted my injury to be their diagnosis. They wanted what most parents want for their children—for them to live a healthy, productive life. They would have taken my burden from me in a heartbeat if they could. Throughout my time at the Center, my parents realized they had to be strong for me, encourage me to fight my way back, and urge me on with their best efforts.

When my father was silent in my room, I knew I must have looked bad because he was usually very vocal. I was hoping my neurologist would say something positive about my diagnosis to my father to help him relax. I was petrified, seeing his distant eyes looking down at me from about ten feet away.

My neurologist leaned over my bed and told me I had a stroke. Extreme measures were taken to keep me alive. I wanted to flick him off with my middle finger, but I did not. I didn't want to hurt his feelings. I made him stop talking with my left hand open, facing him.

I was frightened because I thought only old people had strokes. I knew what was coming because of things I had learned about strokes from studies, TV, and movies. I had tears running from my eyes because I now knew I was severely injured for life. Nothing at all would help me overcome my injury. I was extremely depressed and gave up on myself for a few minutes. All of my hopes, dreams, and yearnings vanished—*poof!* You thought you had a life? Sorry, buddy. You're shit outta luck now. Get over it.

My neurologist had a positive note after he examined me with a reflex hammer (the little hammer the doctor uses to test your reflexes) on my right arm and leg. While I had no feeling in the muscles on my right side, he said that I did show some reflex. I felt I was fortunate because I could have been paralyzed for the rest of my life. This meant I could recover, but he did not know how long it would take or to what extent. His diagnosis was right-side hemiplegia.

A hemiplegic diagnosis is when someone is very weak on one side of the body after a stroke, usually caused by a brain lesion, such as a tumor. Hemiplegic is worse than a hemiparesis diagnosis when someone has a massive stroke. I did not feel any tap on my right-side extremities from the reflex hammer, but I took my neurologist's word, and it gave me hope. Indeed, the mix of emotions during that consult is tough to describe. A roller coaster comes to mind, but that's pretty cliché. Anyway, I suppose any port is good in a storm, so I clung to the doctor's words for dear life.

Is there really hope for me yet?

My neurologist told my parents he did not know how swiftly or to what extent I would recover because medical doctors had little knowledge of what to expect for patients my age. I needed six months of recovery before he could estimate how much of my impaired functions I could get back. My physical, occupational, and speech therapists would play a significant role in assisting me in my recovery for many years.

One month after a massive stroke and global aphasia, a patient should progress rapidly, as the brain tries to heal itself after being severely injured. Three months after a massive stroke, one should continue to improve at a quick pace. After three months, recovery progress will slow down, but it will not stop as long as you continue rehabilitation. Also, after the first few months, things will vary from person to person. Of course, none of this was on my mind at the time of my awakening. That's the thing about having your life turned into some sort of long, sad treatment for an illness that can't really be turned around 100 percent. You become knowledgeable about all kinds of things you wish you didn't know or didn't need to know.

I had seen a picture earlier in my life that said, "Hope reflects belief. Hope believes in the possibilities. Hope rejects cynicism and doubt. People with a higher level of hope believe that though events may not work out fully they will not be defeated. Hope is the dream of a soul awake." I believed in that quote throughout my long recovery, despite the dark moments, and there were many. I think hope and faith in Jesus were vital in terms of my being able to keep a positive attitude for much of the time. Positive outlooks reap positive results in life in general, and when you're in the medical jungle, you need all the help you can get. Staying positive is a big first step.

After my neurologist left my room, the Center's head speech therapist came to make a diagnosis of my verbal ability. She looked into my mouth to see if I could move my tongue side to side and all around. I did all of the exercises she asked me to do. Her diagnosis was I would talk, but she did not know how much I would get back verbally. She told me how to move my tongue to exercise it every day.

I felt relieved when the speech therapist said I would be able to talk because I was unsure. It is very frightening not to be able to express yourself verbally. The next day, using my speech exercises by myself, I was able to say my first word. With very slow, single-letter pronunciation, I said, "MMMooomm," to get my mother's attention. Within a minute, I said short, common words slowly. Some of the words I used frequently were curses I used to say with my friends and during sports activities. Using cuss words made me smile inside for the first time since my surgery. My verbal abilities were going to be very hard to articulate and for others to understand, but my determination and hard work would steer me to a successful recovery.

Aside from the initial evaluation, I had no speech therapists at the Center. They focused on my physical therapy. I practiced speech exercises, on my own, all the time so I could become comfortable talking to others. As I said, it's scary not to be able to communicate with people. You can't just say what you want to say and be understood. It's also hugely, hugely frustrating to be in involuntary silent mode. I couldn't help but picture myself being mute for the rest of my life, despite what my speech therapist said.

Positive outlook, Rob, I'd chide myself when the negative thoughts bubbled up. *Keep the positive. Out with the negative.*

Right after my speech therapist left the room, my new physical therapist came in to put an anti-spasticity hand-immobilization splint on my right forearm and hand, so I would keep my hand open at all times throughout my early recovery. My splint was a resting splint for my paralysis on my right hand and fingers. A resting splint protects from deformities caused by spasms and contractions and stops claw hand (a deformity caused by nerve damage, which results in an unnatural closing of the fingers, resembling a fist).

I was embarrassed about the look of my paralyzed right hand, so I swore I would relearn to use my right fingers. I would work hard on my right hand so my family, friends, and classmates would be able to give me a handshake again. My determination and hard work would prevail in the recovery of my right hand and fingers, but the journey was long and difficult. Of course, I had no idea I'd eventually triumph at the time. I just had to believe I would. For anyone in a dire situation like mine was back then, I can't emphasize enough how important it is to remain positive even when things look like they've gone to hell in a handbasket. With faith and a positive outlook, much progress can be made even when the so-called experts say you're a goner. If they say there's a chance, you've got to believe they might just be right.

Once all of my diagnoses were made, my nurse took me off of my IV and gave me food. I had the Center's famous macaroni and cheese. All over the city, people knew how great the Center's macaroni and cheese was. I would not eat my food because I was not hungry. I was lonely and a little depressed. My neurologist came into my room to try to convince me to eat. He tried to encourage me, saying I would get better with recovery, but he failed. His voice was not commanding, and I blamed him for my severe condition. I believed he was at fault because the surgical date he reserved for my surgery was too late to be successful, even if some of the fault was mine for wanting to play sports.

My neurologist left my room, and a few minutes later, the same neurologist that came to talk to my family a week ago, just after my surgery, came into my room. He sat next to me to convince me to eat. He said I needed to eat or he would put me back on an IV again. My IV was painful with the insertion of the needle, and it would make me fatigued and woozy. His facial expression and bold voice got my attention very fast. No one in my life had ever convinced me like he did that day. He told me I would not recover if I did not have food, so I made myself eat a small amount. I began to eat a little food with each meal, regularly. I gradually improved my food intake, and slowly I started to have increased, modest energy.

From that point on, I tried to succeed in therapy so that I would get better results. That neurologist was like a strict football coach when he instructed me in a compassionate way. I needed to eat to get myself into tip-top shape. He knew how to get patients to do things and knew how to treat them well.

As a side effect of my coma, starting the first night, after my post-diagnosis surgery, I had dreadful hallucinations for a few days. My hallucinations were unusual sensory phenomena experienced after waking from my coma. My hallucinations were frightening episodes of seeing a middle-aged African American nurse come in my room. In my imagination, she would give me a shot in the arm with a big needle that really hurt. I thought she was the devil, so I got my mother to stay overnight in my room for the next couple of nights, until my hallucinations went away.

Friday morning, I had an MRI scan to find out if my neurosurgeon got all of the benign tumor removed, which he did. "Thank God that something actually went right." While I was in the MRI machine, I needed water and ice badly. I was antsy, but I did the best I could to stay still. My surgery was done, but my lengthy physical, occupational, and speech therapies were just beginning.

Later in the morning, my physical therapist came into my room to take me to the Center's physical therapy room. Two nurses lifted me onto a gurney and wheeled me to the therapy room. Once I was there, the same nurses lifted me down onto a mat. When I was on the mat, she told me to move my right arm and leg as much as I could. I could not do what she asked because my right extremities were very weak. She would stretch my right extremities to get my muscles going. Then, after a few days of pulling and extending my right leg with her, I could move my right quadriceps a little. According to stroke.org, "Continued rehabilitation and therapy can help stroke survivors regain voluntary movement even years following their stroke." A week later, after doing arm raises, I felt muscles in my right arm when I tried to move it. I was slowly improving in my therapy.

I felt great moving my muscles on my right extremities. From that point on, I wanted to be in therapy all day long, but my fatigue held me back. My will to walk again grew during weeks of therapy at the Center. My family's support and encouragement helped me to keep improving every day.

My mother was with me every day, for about a month, throughout my stay. When I began my daily therapy, she could not come to help, she would go to the Center's library to research available scientific information about the prognosis for severe brain injuries as a teenager. There was a lack of resources about stroke recovery applicable to a patient my age. She was frustrated about my prognosis and was always searching for concrete information from doctors and research studies to encourage me, my father, my brother, and herself in my recovery.

Whatever little moments of depression my mother felt, at the Center and later in my recovery, she took heart seeing small steps in my improvement. She never stopped encouraging me to recover as much as possible. She didn't know how far I could progress in my recovery, but she had a positive outlook and the patience to encourage me and get me into ongoing therapies that continued for years after I left the Center.

Close to the end of being a patient at the Center, I let a few of my close friends come to visit me. I was in terrible shape and needed more rest for my long journey to recovery. They were crushed looking at me, because I looked weak and sad. I could not communicate with them or be attentive. I wanted them to see me after my successful surgery. I held back from crying because I knew they saw my horrible injury. Never, at any point during my recovery, did they give up on me.

I was so mad I could not even say a sentence to my close friends. It hurt to be with them because of the loss of my speech. I believed they were embarrassed to see me in my bed. They went out of their way to travel to the Center to give me support and encouragement and were unable to do so.

I did not ask my other friends to come visit me, besides those three, because I did not want anyone to find out what happened to me. Turns out they all knew anyway. I was told years later that a few more friends came and visited me, but I was unable to remember things at that time. Memory loss is a symptom of global aphasia. My confidence was extremely low because I was ashamed of myself. My girl relationships were done, I thought, and my popularity was falling, at least in my mind. Essentially, the tumor robbed me of everything I'd ever known and loved. It stole my very identity. I didn't know who this new Rob was or would be, but I definitely knew that nothing in my life would ever be the same again. That realization was profoundly depressing because I'd had a nice life before my brain decided to invite a tumor to set up residence. Now, it seemed at the time, I had nothing but a living hell to endure. Frankly, I wasn't sure if I could make it.

In with the positive ... out with the negative.

CHAPTER 6

Rehabilitation

I needed a tremendous amount of therapy with my injuries. I did not know how difficult and time-consuming my recovery would be in the upcoming months and years. After a month at the Center, my neurologist recommended my parents take me to Marianjoy Rehabilitation Hospital in Wheaton, Illinois, to continue my therapy. Marianjoy was closer to our home, so it would be easier for my family and friends to come and visit me. It had all the therapy programs I needed to help me recover. My parents agreed with my neurologist because of his expertise.

When I was leaving the Center in the ambulance to go to Marianjoy, I was confused. I could not recall why I was leaving the Center, because of my global aphasia, but I was happy I would be close to my home. I wanted to get as far away from the Center as I could. I had horrible memories tied to there in the past month.

I knew about Marianjoy before my surgery. I believed only severely injured patients were there. I was one of those severely injured patients now. I had to bear the thought that I might have to stay at Marianjoy for many weeks or months. My goal was to do the best I could in my therapy in order to go home to be with my family.

My parents waited for me in Marianjoy's lobby until my ambulance arrived. My father had tears in his eyes when I got wheeled, on a gurney, to get to my room. He was very stressed and depressed with what was going on in our lives, but he was excited I was closer to our home. He was hoping I would do the best in my therapies and get back to normal again.

My mother was anxious and upset about my move to Marianjoy. She could not travel in the ambulance with me. She was not allowed to accompany me into my room until the staff had settled me in. She was worried my transfer to Marianjoy would be upsetting to me because of my state of mind.

I was terrified by my arrival to Marianjoy because I was in a new place with new surroundings. Once I checked in and reorganized myself in my new room, I was relieved. Marianjoy was not hectic, with people coming and going every few minutes in my room, like the Center was. I was not depressed about being there because I wanted to get the best therapy with the best opportunity for success. Later that night, my nurse came to help my roommate. He was lying in his bed behind the curtain. She opened the curtain, and I looked at him. He was more severely injured than me. He was in a vegetative state, not able to speak or move.

After seeing him, even though I did feel sorry for him, I felt better about my own situation.

I was ready to work even harder in all of my therapies at Marianjoy—more than I did at the Center. I would give my best efforts to push myself to hit my critical recovery goals because I did not want to be sitting in a wheelchair for the rest of my life. I wanted to be able to have a great conversation with my family and friends again. My determination and hard work helped me through these times. I did not want increasing depression in my future. Sometimes, you have to make a conscious decision not to feel bad, angry, or sad. Sometimes, you have to willfully summon the positive energy that exists within the universe, within us all, to overcome the pervading darkness that accompanies severe medical and mental issues. I strongly believe that my decision to remain positive, despite all the negative energy I could've embraced, led me to the better place I am in today as a result.

My first day at Marianjoy, my nurse helped me to move around. She helped me do stuff—stuff most people do not think about doing when they are getting ready in the morning and throughout the day. For example, getting up out of bed, washing up, using the restroom, changing clothes, putting on shoes, and tying them. Being helped by someone else could have been a routine I would need to get used to for the rest of my life, but I was confident it would not be.

The first item on my agenda, in my therapy that morning, was to see my new neuropsychologist, Scott. Over weeks of my therapy, he helped me improve my lifestyle by encouraging and supporting my ongoing recovery. He helped my damaged, short-term memory and cognitive ability by doing concentrated intervention techniques, research strategies, and neurological examinations and understanding the effects of my neuropsychological conditions on my behavior changes.

When I came into the neuropsychologist's office for the first time, I was surprised he was so young. I was expecting him to be older. I did not think he could be experienced with my condition. Scott changed my view when he introduced himself.

He gave me a friendly smile, so I felt relaxed and was able to trust him with my emotional therapies. He told me I could call him by his first name. Calling him by his first name was a big leap in our relationship. It made me feel he was not above me in his stature in life.

I saw Scott many times while I was at Marianjoy. One time, I told him my relationships with girls were ruined because of my inability to have a good conversation with them and my physical condition. Scott told me to be positive. I would find someone who cared for me and gave support in my recovery. A large number of people would look at me not as a person with a lasting injury but as a great person who battled and succeeded in my recovery there at Marianjoy. All I needed to do was work hard in my therapies to recover as much as possible.

Scott was always optimistic about my life, and my depression got better with many counseling sessions over the next few years. He gave me new recovery goals to accomplish so I would increase my confidence in doing sports and activities in my new life. He gave me valuable advice and initiatives as I was working toward going back to my high school for my senior year. Scott reminded me I still had my family's love, support, and encouragement in my recovery, through this tough time.

About two months after arriving at Marianjoy, near the end of my stay, Scott spoke with my mother. He said, even if I had to go through such a devastating accident again, I possessed the right stuff to deal with it. He said I listened intently, thought genuinely, and understood how to focus on life goals, despite my severe condition. My strength of character would make me successful going forward.

I felt my physical therapy was the most important activity at Marianjoy. My new physical therapist, Brett, was energetic and encouraging. He was my favorite therapist in all of my recovery. He pushed me to do my best in therapy sessions. He made me do a lot of stretching and balancing techniques so I would be able to control my own body. I needed to be flexible when I began to exercise. Stretching was crucial and my first step in my early recovery.

I did more therapy exercises and got more strength in the first few days at Marianjoy than I did in one month at the Center. I was fatigued at the Center because of my injury. I knew if I worked hard at Marianjoy, I would be able to stand up on my feet, walk, and jog again.

I did active exercises, and my physical effort developed into muscular activity. I worked on a range of motion to get my muscles moving. During my recovery, active rehabilitation exercises helped me strengthen the neural pathways and create new connections in my brain that enabled me to perform the movement. It's important to understand that when neural pathways are destroyed, the brain can actually reroute the pathways, but it takes time for that to happen. Although the progress was slow, it was measurable, and my confidence about my future increased. When I regained enough movement, I continued improving the function in my right extremities every day. I looked at that as the first big step—that and being able to talk effectively again.

Early on in my stay, my parents became very involved in my rehabilitation with Brett. My mother was there every night, and my father came on weekends to encourage me to work hard in therapies. My parents were concerned when they learned there was no therapy on weekends. They asked Brett what they could do to continue my physical treatments when he was gone. He recommended lifting my right leg as a therapy exercise so I could get my motor functions back. My parents would help me move my muscles and joints through their full range of motion. Range of motion is the measurement of the amount of movement around a specific joint or body part.

The next Saturday, my parents lifted my right leg gently and bent it at my knee. They pushed my leg toward my torso and asked if I felt any pain. I did not. My parents were unsure of themselves because they had never done this before and thought they might hurt me. They kept working with my right leg, and I could push against them a little. My mother called down to the physical therapy room in the basement for more guidance on what to do next. It turned out Brett was there that morning and would be up around noon.

When Brett got to my room, my parents were still working with me, and he was shocked at what he saw. He said he did not know I could participate in this therapy exercise. He did not think I could push with my right leg this well. Brett changed everything in my current therapy plan and was looking forward to Monday's exercise. I made a significant impact and milestone on my physical abilities because of the strength in my right leg.

That week, in the morning, before I left with Brett from my room in my wheelchair, I told him I would stand up from my bed by myself, and I did! I started to stroll, taking small steps at a time, with his help, to the therapy room. A week later, I did not want help walking. I began walking alone, bracing myself against the wall with my left hand. I had more strength in my right leg from the past week because of my determination and hard work.

I told my mother my walk took a lot of time and energy out of me, but I was definitely on my way to a tremendous physical recovery! I had accomplished my main recovery goal: to walk. My next recovery goal was to be able to jog. I kept believing I would be normal again through the encouragement of my therapists throughout my stay.

Each Sunday, from the beginning to the end of my stay, I got to go home to relax on my bed but only for the day. The first time, I was back I was in a wheelchair, and my father pushed me into our house. I saw my dog, Biscuit, a yellow Labrador, and I gave her a huge hug. She came up to take a nap with me in my bed. When I woke, my family and close friends came to visit me and provided encouragement about my recovery.

When my visitors left, I was depressed because I was not staying at home for good. I wanted to be like my friends again. They were able to walk correctly and have conversations with others. On the way back to Marianjoy, I felt less confident and unstable with my feelings again. My mother and I stopped for a bite to eat at a burger restaurant I love. When we went into the fast-food restaurant, it was almost empty, with no other customers. It was nine o'clock at night, and their maintenance worker was mopping the inside floor. He looked like he hated his job. When we were almost done eating, I told her I wanted to die because I could not deal with the loss of my old life.

My mother started to talk to me about the concept of building and experiencing a new life for myself. She believed, in time, if I kept working and meeting recovery goals, I would discover a great new life. She wanted me to know my adversity could bring me a deeper appreciation of what I have, new horizons, enduring faith, and a greater understanding of myself and others. She believed my gradual recognition of my strength, determination, and confidence would lead me to my fabulous new life.

My mother's motivational speech had a significant impact on me. I got more determination to keep going every day in my therapies. I cherished my time with her more from then on. To see me suffer, if I gave up on my therapies, would destroy her inside. I got more confidence and self-esteem in myself because of her. I could do anything I wanted. I just needed to try harder than ever to meet my goals. I wanted to prove to others that, while I may have a lasting injury, I would set and accomplish my goals.

Monday morning, about a month and a half after I came out of the coma, my mother, who kept my balance when I was doing my daily tasks to get ready for therapy, saw my muscles on my lower right leg move uncontrollably for the first time. She was very excited! She read a memoir while I was at the Center, and the author had spasms that led to his recovery, allowing him to walk again.

My brain's ability to heal and rewire itself intensified because of spasms. It was rapidly trying to heal itself, resulting in noticeable improvement on my right-side paralysis in the first few months of my recovery. After a few months, the speed of my recovery, by spasms, slowed down a little, but my brain would never stop trying to restore and improve itself.

My mother told my head medical doctor at Marianjoy about my spasms. He examined me by having me stand up, holding on to Brett's arm, and do critically essential exercises. He saw me moving my right leg uncontrollably. He was very excited for me because my brain was causing these spasms. My spasms were a sign of my right leg coming back from my injury, according to him.

My right arm began having spasms a few days later, and my confidence rose even more. I had spasms often during the day and at night. I was getting better therapy exercise results. My spasms were a boost of motivation to help give me a great workout.

A few days later, my right arm was moving more, but it was still fragile, so my physical therapist had me start doing bench presses on the weight machine. I could not move my right fingers outward, but I could squeeze the weight bar. Both sides of my arms were doing the work because my right arm muscles would follow the motions of my left arm, causing reconnections in my brain. Eventually, he would make me lift dumbbells with both my right and left arms, with his help, because I was gaining more strength.

That week, one night, I woke up because I had to go to the bathroom. Each time I got up from sleeping, I would hit a button attached to my bed to get my nurse to help me walk to the bathroom. This time was different. I walked to the bathroom with no supervision. I had to work hard to push myself with my right leg to make me move successfully, but I accomplished another recovery goal.

I did not need a nurse or physical therapists anymore to move my body because I could walk. I knew my right leg was going to be a severe emotional and physical workout, but I could handle it. Another recovery goal I set for myself was not to have a limp in my right foot. Setting goals is essential in life and in business. Without a clear objective to strive toward, it's typical for people to fall into a state of inertia. That inertia leads to depression. A purposeful life is a rewarding life, and, for me, my sole purpose was to beat the beast that my brain unleashed on me when that internal carotid artery branch burst and blood filled my skull like a mini swimming pool.

Later in the morning, Brett came into my room to take me to therapy. I told him I walked to the bathroom by myself last night and used the wall as my support. It took a lot out of me, but I succeeded. He was in awe and congratulated me! He let me walk to the therapy room, with his support going down the stairs, to boost my confidence and self-esteem for my crucial exercises.

Each day after my physical therapy session, I went to see Amy, my occupational therapist, for my session with her. The main difference between occupational therapy and physical therapy is that occupational therapy focuses on improving a client's ability to perform activities of daily living. Physical therapy focuses on improving a client's ability to perform movement of the human body.

I worked on getting my right fingers to open up one finger at a time because of my spasticity. My spasticity, or continued contraction, was the main culprit of my stiff right hand. My root cause of spasticity was my brain-muscle miscommunication. My right-hand muscles got tense and tight because they could not receive signals from my brain like they once did before my stroke. So, even though my brain was trying to tell my hand muscles to relax, my muscles couldn't hear that command. It's a bit like a pilot trying to communicate with the control tower, but the coms are down, and there's nothing but smoke signals to go on. Not good. Not a good place at all. But I still had hope. I still kept hard at achieving the goals I set for myself, and I always moved the bar higher and higher all on my own.

To fix my brain-muscle communication, I did specific exercises with my right hand to rewire the connections in my brain, using its neuroplasticity. Neuroplasticity is the brain's ability to form and reorganize synaptic connections following an injury. I did them very repetitively. The more I repeated my exercises, the stronger my brain-muscle communications became. I retrained my brain to control my hand muscles through repetitive rehabilitation exercise. By performing exercises over and over, I was fixing the communication between my brain and muscles. Over time, my muscles slowly learned to open and relax.

Amy held my right fingers outward to stretch and massage them. She carefully let my right fingers slowly retract so I would not injure my right hand. To help my right fingers open up more, she used a neuromuscular electrical stimulation (NMES) device. It worked! An NMES is a device that sends electrical impulses to muscles in the body—in my case, my right fingers. This input caused my right finger muscles to extend. Electrical stimulation helped retrain my right finger muscles to function by increasing strength and range of motion.

NMES helped my right fingers open up, but I had a long way to go in my therapy before I could give a proper handshake. My right fingers were the most difficult to exercise, of all the right extremities. It was frustrating because there was no weightlifting involved. The only thing I could do was leave my right fingers open at all times and pick up small, light items, hoping to get my brain to reconnect.

My speech therapist, Lisa, helped me to relearn how to pronounce words, understand others, ask questions, organize thoughts, pay attention, remember, plan, and problem-solve. I was not enthused about seeing her because she was too dull, but I knew it was crucial to my therapy. I reminded myself I needed to be perfect in my conversations, so no one would ask what happened to me or what was wrong with me.

At this point in my early recovery, it had become painfully obvious that I had to basically start all over again in terms of the basics in life, like walking, talking, and even thinking straight. The enormity of the task sometimes overwhelmed me. Depression would set in. Out would go the positive, and in would come the negative. It was only when I made the conscious choice to recognize this when it was happening that I could take active mental and emotional steps to reverse the process. In a sense, I was asserting control over my emotions so that I could assert control over my entire life. It was an amazing realization, one that continues to shape me as the man I now am. Your emotions can hold you back, or they can rocket you forward to achieve even the toughest objectives.

I found out on my own that I could sing songs at Marianjoy. Singing songs was not as difficult as talking and helped me in my speech recovery. When I had a massive stroke, I was unable to speak, so I sang songs to practice my language in the early part of my recovery. I felt proud of singing songs because I used words I was unable to use correctly in speech.

Toward the end of my stay at Marianjoy, my sexual

desires came back. I saw a beautiful, young, female therapist who kept looking at me as she passed the doorway to my room while I was resting for the day. She had a great smile, which made me happy because I loved making people smile before my injury. I could have said hi or smiled back, but my confidence and self-esteem were not high enough. I felt handsome again, but I needed to keep healing from my emotional scars. I started to believe I could have relationships with girls once I was done recovering. All I needed was more confidence and self-esteem to push me to ask them out on dates in the future.

I was surprised when my girlfriend from high school, Tracy, and a mutual friend came to visit me. I was nervous she might judge me for having a lasting injury. They saw me in a wheelchair, a right hand-immobilization splint, and barely talking. When they left, I knew I had to focus more on my verbal recovery because I could hardly communicate with them. That was the last time Tracy and I would have a conversation. I did see Tracy a few other times in my life, but each time, I was nervous and kept my distance from her. I would never reconnect with her.

To make me feel better after the disastrous visit with Tracy, I considered my roommate's severe, traumatic brain injury. He did not get any support, encouragement, or get-well cards throughout the time I was with him. I was amazed and inspired how many friends I had in high school because there were hundreds of get-well cards I received from students and teachers. They gave me encouragement to recover. It felt good to know people cared, and I was getting more confident my recovery would succeed and I would be normal again.

I felt sorry for patients who did not see any gains from

their recovery efforts at Marianjoy. I believed some of the survivors were depressed and gave up on themselves. I saw some patients in the physical therapy room who would not try to push themselves to get better, as I did. I saw a woman who had a severe injury to her right leg. She had large metal pins to help stabilize her recovery. I could see she had given up after what happened to her because she was not working hard in therapy.

I understood how easy it would have been for me to give up too. I understood that while I had no choice about my brain blowing an internal carotid artery branch during the operation, just like I'd had no choice about getting a tumor in the first place, I did have a choice as to how I would respond to what life dealt me. I think that how we respond to things really makes a difference in the quality of our lives. Choose to explode in anger, and you'll get negativity. Choose to respond with compassion, sensitivity, and a genuine desire to accomplish a goal with positivity, and that goal will be achieved.

When I was released from Marianjoy inpatient care, in a couple of months, I could slowly walk with a limp and was able to use my right arm to do some movements. My right hand was still almost closed. My speech was improving because I could say short sentences.

I had achieved many of my recovery goals after my injury, and I was ready for more. As I said earlier, three months after a stroke is the tipping point. Progress in recovery will slow down after that, but the recovery will continue with sustained therapeutic exercises. I was determined to keep making progress no matter what it took.

CHAPTER 7

Outpatient Care

My parents decided I should go to Marianjoy's outpatient care facility in St. Charles, Illinois, a nearby town, for two months to continue the improvement in my recovery. At age seventeen, they were hoping I would recover enough to go back to school in the fall. I was excited, as I had proven I could make big strides in my recovery, but I did not want my friends to see me yet. I wanted to improve more with my recovery. The outpatient facility had all the recovery equipment that the inpatient hospital had, so I could improve while staying at home.

I was happy to be home for good so that I could be with my family. I knew how important a close family was because I had gone so long without living with mine. I had missed my dog, Biscuit, because she would always cuddle with me in my bed and was a psychologist who listened to my feelings about girl problems. When you're seventeen, you're not fully formed as an adult. Your brain is still developing, in fact, and that meant that I was operating from a rather unique position. Hell, I'd had a massive stroke in my teens, something medical researchers had not studied much. My insecurities about relationships with the opposite sex were normal. My condition just made the feelings more intense.

My parents did not have to take me to the outpatient care facility. Marianjoy had a special bus that picked me up each morning and dropped me back off in the late afternoon, after my therapy sessions. The only thing my parents had to do was get me out of my bed. Getting out of bed was tough on me because of my anti-seizure side effects. They made me fatigued every day, even though I took a couple of naps in the afternoon. My fatigue decreased my energy and concentration and influenced my emotional and psychological health.

The outpatient care facility surroundings were not as busy as the inpatient care facility. There were about fifteen patients, and they were not as severely injured as the patients at the inpatient care facility. All of them were walking, speaking fine, and did not look depressed. Most of them did not need extra help from a daily nurse to do things. They seemed attentive to what the therapist was instructing them to do. I was in the worst condition of all the patients there at that time.

My therapists were friendly and easy to get along with. They did not make me nervous when we had conversations about my therapy instructions and things I liked to do. They gave me support and encouragement to work hard toward gaining more strength. My recovery exercises were exhausting, but I never gave up. Instead, I asked my therapists if I could have more therapy sessions with them. They said absolutely.

The outpatient physical therapy room was small compared to the physical therapy room at the inpatient hospital. There were only three windows where the two treadmills and elliptical were. The most important recovery exercise my physical therapist, Stephanie, gave me was moving my right arm when I walked by holding two six-foot-long, brown, wood poles, two inches in width, with both my arms. She would move the long poles toward and away from her as we walked. This movement helped me walk and keep my balance without support. I was walking the best I had since my surgery.

Soon after, I accomplished another one of my recovery goals by jogging slowly in the grass. It was still difficult getting my right foot not to stumble. I would jog at home on weekends, a little bit, so that I could get into shape again, just as I'd been before my brain surgery. One of my recovery goals was to come back and be competitive again in sports. I knew I could not play football because of my brain surgery, and basketball was tough, having to shoot and dribble the ball with my right hand. My recovery goal was to play baseball again.

My new occupational therapist, Bonnie, helped my right fingers every day, making improvements slowly compared to my right leg movements. At the end of my stay, my right fingers were able to open up enough so I could walk without some people noticing I was partially paralyzed in my right hand. I believed I would be able to give a handshake within a few months because of my therapy exercises. I kept my anti-spasticity hand-immobilization splint on at night when I was sleeping to keep my right fingers open when I was resting.

My speech therapy was improving considerably. I did more word pronunciation recovery exercises to strengthen my annunciation so no one would be confused about what I was saying. Before my injury, my word pronunciation and word finding were easy when I was talking to people. After my injury, I was very angry at myself because I had huge speech problems. When someone spoke, it took a long time for me to process what they said. I could not come up with my responses fast enough. By the time I understood what they were saying, oftentimes they had moved on to a new topic. It was a vicious, infuriating circle.

I had conversations with a few patients to improve my word-finding skills and relearn how to retrieve and ask questions. I was proud of my speech recovery at the end of my stay, and I was building more confidence to talk to a couple of people I ran into in my hometown.

I received encouragement in my therapy from other patients, and they became my new friends. Some of them let me into their personal lives by telling me stories about their family members and friends who were worse off than me. One patient told me an awful story about her son who was killed from a gunshot to the chest. He was in the wrong place at the wrong time. While they did open up about some things, the patients did not like talking about what had happened to them. This shows how hard it is to deal with an injury. Their heartbreaking stories helped me during my recovery because I had a second chance I was going to cherish from now on.

I left the outpatient care facility in the summer because I wanted to stay at home and rest in the mornings. This meant I would have new private therapists in my hometown. I did all the therapy exercises they asked me to do, but my recovery was slowing down. I did not give up though, because of my will to improve as much as possible. Besides, I'd been warned that progress would slow, even with continuous therapy. The brain simply works in mysterious ways. I now know far more than I ever wanted to about brains and all that related stuff. Such is the way of it when your brain goes nuts on you and then the surgery goes sideways.

At the end of June, I had an appointment with my neurologist. He discovered I had made a lot of recovery in the six months since my surgery in January. He changed my hemiplegic diagnosis to a hemiparesis diagnosis. I had weakness on the right side of my body. I moved my right-side extremities more than a hemiplegic victim did, according to him. Hearing this downgraded diagnosis made me feel awesome! I knew I would be able to accomplish more recovery goals.

I believed my spasms were a huge key to my recovery because I had gained a tremendous amount of muscle strength during the past months. I asked my neurologist how long my recovery would take, and he said it would be years, not months. It depended upon how much unwavering dedication I had to continue my rehabilitation exercises.

He also determined that my global aphasia was greatly improved and downgraded that diagnosis to just aphasia. The doctor was impressed by my recovery. Even though he told me my recovery would take years, I left his office with great optimism and knew I had the unwavering dedication he mentioned.

I would try to prove to anyone who might have thought I couldn't do it that they were wrong by doing more therapy exercises and crushing my recovery goals. I improved more with my ambitions over the summer. My injury would not get the best of me, because I was a fighter, not a quitter. My inner strength to overcome my stroke came from my father. He had been raised in a low-income family, yet he got an athletic scholarship from an excellent university and succeeded in his life because he worked hard in sports.

I believed some people would curl up and literally die because of their recovery depression. They could not do things they used to do before their injury. I would succeed because of my continued desire to meet my recovery goals, despite my injury and depression. I found that simply listening to my therapists and following their advice worked. It isn't possible to skip to the end. You have to focus on the exercise given (no matter how small) and do your best to improve that exercise. With that focus, you can improve that exercise, which will lead to another. Have faith in the process. It may not be easy to keep the faith when times are at their darkest, but if you can manage to do it, you'll find that the world will become a brighter place for you than if you don't.

I asked my neurologist if I could stop using the splint. It was a device that reminded me of my horrific accident. He said I could get a squishy ball, in lieu of the splint, when I fell asleep, to make sure I did not let my right hand close. I believed if I did not use my squishy ball when I fell asleep, most of my therapy exercises would be lost. I would hold on to the squishy ball every night from then on. At the beginning of the night, my hand would squeeze the ball tightly, of its own accord. When I would wake in the morning, my hand was a bit more relaxed. I still use that same ball every night.

My new occupational therapist, Jenny, did the same thing as my occupational therapists at Marianjoy, both inpatient and outpatient. I was confident I would be able to accomplish my recovery goal with my fingers, but it would take longer than I thought. On my own, I kept my right fingers open when I sat down and rested to prevent them from retracting because of my spasticity. If I did not keep my hand open and make it move all the time, my spasticity would get worse in my right hand, according to my neurologist.

I had sessions with my new speech therapist, Ann, in Yorkville, the next town over from Oswego. I went two times a week to practice saying difficult words, continue improving my comprehension, and practice asking people questions. I wanted my friends and classmates to be able to understand me. I still had trouble in group conversations, but I was improving slowly. I was determined to be able to think of responses and verbalize them in my conversations someday soon.

My new physical therapist, Emily, did similar exercises as my past physical therapists. She helped me grow more muscle by making me push on her body with my right leg and stretch it. I was exhausted in sessions with her, but my right leg and limp were not as noticeable when my senior year began, except when I was nervous or it was cold outside.

When I was not with my therapists, my brother took over. He was staying at home to take a few courses at our community college in the summer while he was attending Knox College in Galesburg, Illinois, a small college away from our town. My brother would jog with me to make sure I did it the right way, despite my partial paralysis. When I would run for any length of time, my right hand would relax and start to open, but he wanted me to close it to match my good hand. I wanted to look like a regular jogger without my hand loosely flopping about. My brother would remind me to lift my right quadriceps so I would not stumble when I was exhausted from jogging. I stumbled a lot on the high school track. He was annoying, but he encouraged me to keep jogging to improve my right extremities and endurance.

I began to become irritated by my brother because I wanted to jog by myself and be independent. I didn't want him to keep giving me instructions on what to do next. I needed to meditate because of my stress and focus on what my friends would think of me when I joined them in my upcoming senior year. I used these thoughts to keep me going and working hard. Although he had the best intentions, my brother made that difficult.

This sort of thing is common in situations like mine. While we can all empathize with someone who has suffered a terrible stroke, we can't get inside the head of that person to really know what he or she is thinking and feeling. As a result, we say and do things that really piss the person off sometimes, and we don't even know it. The best advice is to listen more than offering your own two cents all the time. Quiet, laid-back, and sensitive support will do wonders for the person in question.

Over the summer, I impressed my brother with my determination and hard work in my training. I became independent from him by being persistent in telling him he needed to let me do things on my own.

One day, my brother and I were working out on our high school track, and a few of my friends and classmates were watching me from a distance. I later discovered they were amazed at the sight of me jogging because they thought I would be in a wheelchair or aided by a helper. They had no information besides what happened to me during and right after my surgery. Some of those classmates did not even know I had brain surgery that caused my partial paralysis. Those friends did not visit me when I was recovering in late winter and spring, so they didn't know how much I had improved.

When I heard they were watching me jog, I was proud of the number of recovery improvements I had made. I had endured six months of concentrated physical therapy to become stronger and considerably diminish my right-sided paralysis.

Concerning my mental ability in high school after my surgery, I had to get help from two teachers in the summer, my father and another teacher. I had to pass the spring courses of my junior year that I'd missed because of my therapy. I leaned heavily on my teachers. My father put in a lot of time that summer making sure I could pass his class. I still had a lot of difficulty with the skills needed to read, write, and learn. I needed to improve so I would be ready and equipped for my senior year.

I did not want to return to high school for an extra year because I had fewer friends in classes below mine. I had a tough time concentrating on learning new material, but I was determined to finish my past courses. Before my injury, I had good grades because I would focus on working hard on all of my assignments, and I studied well for exams. My senior-year recovery goal was to study hard to get my diploma and go on to get a higher-education degree.

One reason I kept improving in my recovery was just before my senior year started, I went to a brain injury support group in the same place I was an outpatient. I saw many victims of various kinds of brain injuries, and many of them would not participate in our support group conversation, including me. I was nervous because I was lost in our discussions about the problems and issues we'd had to go through since our injuries.

What turned my way of thinking was seeing a teenage victim, about the same age as me, who did not participate at all. After our first meeting, my mother talked to his mother about why he did not speak. He did not seem to have anything wrong with his verbal ability. She said this was the first social meeting her son had attended since his brain injury happened about six months ago. He was ashamed about what had happened to him and opposed any attempt to socialize with other brain injury survivors and family members.

I was mad at her son because he could talk with ease but I had difficulty getting out a sentence to our group. I got lost trying to find the right words I was attempting to say most of the time. I felt his mother did not take any serious action to get him out of his emotional coma until then. I believed she had no guidance from her family members, friends, or medical staff.

They had a significant impact on me, which caused my emotional feelings to heal more that night. I tried my hardest to have conversations with our support group victims, their families, and my friends from then on. I decided to be less irritable and emotionally aggressive in my family conversations about our problems and issues. I finally learned that to agree with my parents, I had to be obedient and calm, to talk things out peacefully.

Near the end of my summer break, my family congratulated me for my hard work because I overcame a large number of obstacles over the many months since my injury. They let me go watch the Colorado Rockies versus the Chicago Cubs at Wrigley Field. My cousin Mike set up a meeting with Joe, the all-star player I had talked to prior to my surgery. Mike was there because he was covering the Rockies for the season again.

My parents were worried about me getting lost but in the end agreed I could go since I would be accompanied by my uncle and brother. My uncle drove us to Wrigley Field and parked in the VIP parking. When we got to the Wrigley Field gates, I felt secure with them. Even though I was worried I might get lost in the crowd at the game, I knew I would be okay.

I met Joe at the infield fence on the away team's side of the field before the game. Ten seconds went by, and suddenly about ten children and teenagers were around us, asking Joe for an autograph. He opened the gate to let me come onto the baseball field to talk to him about my recovery and goals. Normally, he would take the time to acknowledge his fans, but at that point, he was focused on me. I felt great because I believed I was his biggest fan in that moment.

I got to shake Joe's hand with my right hand, but it was tough opening my right fingers. I had a lot of trouble with my pronunciation and word-finding skills in our conversation because I was nervous talking to a famous ballplayer. Unfortunately, because of my aphasia, almost immediately, I had no memory of what he said, but I was inspired by the interaction. As I was leaving, I told him I would be fully recovered if I met him again in the future. He was positive and nice, but we did not get another opportunity to meet. I felt great that day, and my confidence was rising, and I was less depressed because not many baseball fans get to meet an all-star, have a private conversation with him on Wrigley Field, and get his encouragement to keep recovering.

My father was happy I got to meet Joe and saw that my confidence and self-esteem improved from then on. Before my senior year began, he asked my varsity football coach if I could join their football team as an emotional leader. He told him that I deserved recognition for all of the things I'd had to do in my recovery to get back into high school.

I did not want to be on the football team because I could not play, but my family convinced me to change my mind by giving me more support and encouragement. They were proud of me for not giving up on myself and wanted people to know I was recovering. I agreed and joined the team because I felt proud of my recovery achievements.

CHAPTER 8

Senior Year

I remember walking into my high school on the first day of my senior year. I came to school late in the morning because I was still fatigued from the anti-seizure medicine. I was nervous about seeing my friends, classmates, and teachers for the first time since my injury.

During that week, Scott, my neuropsychologist from Marianjoy, agreed to come to my high school to talk to a few of my close friends about my injury in detail. He told them not to give up on me because I was still recovering and making progress. I would have a great life, but I needed support so I would not get depressed over my past.

My close friend Tom had visited me at the Center when I was in the coma. Over time, he became my best friend because he cared for me deeply. He was also brilliant. I believed the most intelligent and mature of my friends were the most compassionate. Tom would always have time for me when I needed more support and encouragement. I would often get depressed my senior year, but he was there to cheer me up. He would call me to come out with him to parties and get together with friends.

One time, Tom convinced me to come out with him and our friends. They were going to go skating on a pond outdoors. He told me I needed to come even though I couldn't skate. I could still hang and have a great time. It was during the winter. I remember there was snow on the ground, and it was moderately cold for northern Illinois. As my friends laced up their skates, I was jealous of their ability to go skating but was glad I had joined them. I was happy to be around friends and not stuck in my room, moping at home.

In early spring of my senior year, I went with one of my close friends to a party on a Saturday night. My friend and I were stopped by a cop, and he asked why my friend was speeding and where he was going. I was the passenger, and the cop asked me a question. I was nervous and scared because he could take me to jail if he wanted to. I had trouble saying sentences. Luckily, my friend explained my condition. For doing that, I looked up to him from then on, more than most of my close friends. I was ashamed and angry at myself because I had so much trouble conversing with the cop.

In my senior year, academic courses were hard, so I went to the learning disability (LD) classroom to get help. The learning disability teacher helped me understand my homework and learn strategies for reading struggles so that I could graduate and prosper. Getting a high grade point average (GPA) was not a reality anymore. My recovery goal was to pass all of my courses and graduate on time in May 1996.

I knew I was intelligent, despite my severely damaged short-term memory. Before my injury, I thought LD students were significantly less intelligent than other students their age. Throughout my senior year, I realized the LD students were slow at learning, but many were very intelligent. Many had learning disabilities from injuries like mine, but some were born with them. It didn't make them less intelligent but often meant they had to learn in different ways from the average student.

During football games in the fall, I felt embarrassed walking to our sidelines before the game and after the game, especially later in the season. It was cold outside, which made my right-side spasticity worse, making walking even more difficult. I felt like everyone was watching me when I walked, judging me as a person who they felt sorry for at the game. I did not put on my football jersey, number 81, because in my opinion, I did not deserve it. Before my accident, I was a good athlete, and now I could not catch a football properly. I felt I was not a part of our team. I wasn't even playing. Even though I was an emotional leader, I didn't feel I was worthy of the jersey.

In the spring, I decided to be on the baseball team as an emotional leader and a player. I began getting more strength and endurance when we did drills, and I jogged when we practiced. In our games, I did not get to be on the defense because of my weak skull and partial paralysis. If I were to get hit by a fast baseball in the head, it would likely cause a grand mal seizure.

I did get to bat a few times in the season as a pinch hitter. My bat swing was slow compared to my bat swing before my injury, but I could grip the bat despite my hand spasticity. Also, my eye-hand coordination was okay, so I was ready.

The score was not close, so being at bat did not do harm or cause complaints from any of our players. My father, who came to some of my home games, and I were very scared and nervous when I was up to bat. The opposing pitcher could hit me in the head with the ball. I did have a helmet on my head, but I did not want a grand mal seizure.

With my willpower, I was ready to get a hit. Even though I had the will, I was nervous and scared, as this was the first competitive thing I had done since my surgery. I really was just hoping I could make contact with the ball. I swung at the first pitch, which was a fast ball down the middle. I couldn't believe it, but I made contact, and at first, I thought it would be a hit over the first baseman's head. Unfortunately, the first baseman took a step back and was able to catch the ball. I was proud when I hit the baseball because I felt I was contributing to our team.

Toward the end of the season, an incident happened when one of our players commented on an African American player on the opposing team. He called him the N-word. I was agitated at him because I respect African Americans the same as I do Caucasian people. I gave him a speech about how wrong he was, even though speaking was difficult for me. I felt proud of myself for standing up to him when no one else on our team did.

Close to the end of school, I got to meet Bob Love, a former professional basketball player and star for the Chicago Bulls, at a junior high school in my town. The player rose as one of the most sought-after motivational speakers in the country. I listened to his speech about how he overcame his most formidable opponent—his stuttering—as he spoke to all of the students in the school gym. He emphasized the importance of getting an education and reaching goals that were a challenge for him in his childhood and professional basketball career.

After his speech, I had a conversation with Mr. Love to congratulate him on his accomplishments over his lifetime. I tried my hardest to have a reasonable discussion and told him he talked smoothly. He did not hide his disability; instead, he embraced it to show others you could do anything you put your mind to. I got more confidence in my "disability" because it is just a word. I wanted to be a motivational speaker just like him.

During my senior year, I had improved more at comprehension and language skills in my everyday conversations just by talking to my friends and classmates. I did not go to speech therapies because I did not think I needed it. If I had, I would have improved my speaking skills even more over that time. Looking back, I regret that I got overconfident and didn't go, because I am sure I would have benefited from further sessions.

At the end of my senior year, I arm-wrestled my friend Joey, superstar fullback on our football team, in our science class. I was intimidated by him, physically because of his strength, but I trusted him not to crush my right hand and arm. When we wrestled, I had more power in my right arm. I didn't win, but I did feel like my strength had increased. I was improving more.

My physical therapy sessions suffered because I was so busy with school, fatigued from my medication and simply wanted to hang with my friends. If I had put extra work into my physical therapy, I could have improved more than I did. My recovery and strength in my right extremities could have improved more, but I did not use our school's weight room to exercise. My medicine was a big factor because I was tired, which led to me taking naps throughout the day in the nurse's office. I regret that I did not push through my fatigue and work harder.

I graduated from high school in May because I passed all my courses! My parents were delighted because of all I had done my senior year. They convinced me I should have a graduation party to celebrate my success. My mother called two of my mentors from Marianjoy, Scott and Brett, because they helped me in the central part of my recovery.

I did not want to have a graduation party because I did not know if my friends would come when I invited them. I decided only my close friends would get an invitation. They gave me more support and encouragement throughout my whole recovery. Almost everyone I invited showed up. I was surprised I was able to converse and respond well with each one of my family and friends for a short time. When my guests left, they were smiling at me. I believed I had recovered more than they expected. I was ready for whatever would happen next in my future journey.

I was too nervous to have a conversation with any female students during the senior year, besides a few. Because of this, I did not ask anyone to the homecoming dance or prom. I thought they might say no if I asked them out on a date because I needed more confidence. I was afraid to ask my guy friends to be my wingman so that I would not be so nervous with female students.

But many positive things happened during my senior-year activities. I was honored by my friends and classmates who voted me homecoming king in the fall. I was asked by a female friend to go to homecoming. I said yes because I wouldn't have to ask anyone and could still go with a date. We had a great time all night long.

I did not go to the prom for similar reasons. After my senior year, I talked to a different close female friend, and she said she would have been proud to go with me to prom. She respected me for staying in school and fighting through my emotional adjustments. I regret not having been more confident and bolder when it came to talking to girls and my friends.

Another thing I did was get my driver's license back by passing an approved examination concerning my vision, rules of the road, and physical coordination at Marianjoy's driver-testing department. Certain people with seizures would not get their driver's license because they had problems with consciousness, awareness, or control of movement. I passed all of these. When I graduated, I was walking on my right leg with no limp—maybe a little if I started to get nervous.

Throughout the year, my friends gave me support and hung out with me some weekends, but I suffered from my damaged word-finding skills, the ability to respond correctly, and comprehension in a conversation. After we graduated, I was upset at my friends. They left me and went on with their lives. Because of my aphasia, I did not understand that a lot of high school friends break apart after their senior year. A few years later, I realized why they left. Most went to college and left to improve their lives. I finally was able to realize their leaving had nothing to do with me. I felt silly for thinking they had gone out of their way to leave me. I let many of them go, and we did not keep in touch. Much later in my life, technology and social media allowed me to reconnect with them.

During the late spring of 1996, when I was eighteen, about two weeks after I graduated from high school, I had a grand mal seizure. I forgot to take my medicine for a couple of days. My mother was my nurse, and she forgot to give me my anti-seizure dosages, which caused my grand mal seizure. I did not blame my mother because she had her own life and many other responsibilities. I should have remembered to take my dosages myself.

My grand mal seizure began when I got up from my bed in the morning and went to the bathroom. I didn't feel it right when I woke up. I don't know why. In fact, I always had so much pain that the little things didn't bother me so much. I heaved myself out of bed, walked in my bare feet to the bathroom, did my business, and was back in my bedroom, on my way to get dressed, when my right leg began vibrating, trembling, and flexing. Then my left leg joined in. "Oh no." I sat down on the floor to prevent a fall in the very real likelihood that I was having the mother of all seizures. I was right; it was a seizure. In seconds, my whole body was moving, violently, on its own. I could not talk and was in intense pain because of my muscle contractions.

My brother awakened because he heard our dog, Biscuit, whining outside my bedroom door. Then he heard me making strange noises, so he got up from his bed and opened my locked door. I always locked my door because I did not want my mother to come in when I was getting my beauty sleep. I was a light sleeper. He pushed my door, and it opened because it was not a good lock. He found me writhing on the floor. He had never witnessed a grand mal seizure, so he thought I had taken illegal drugs and might be overdosing. He called out to my mother to come quickly.

My parents came right away, and my mother realized

I was having a grand mal seizure. She told my brother and father what was happening. They were scared because I had never had a seizure like this. She told my father to call an ambulance right away. She knew the paramedics would know what to do. She knew not to confine me physically and maneuvered me away from hitting my head near my closet doors. It was almost ten minutes of intense pain.

My mother thought I could not breathe and was deliberating with my family about giving me cardiopulmonary resuscitation (CPR), but before she could, I made a weird sound that indicated I could breathe. I was thankful she did not have to give me CPR. I did not want to be kissed by my mother on the lips for a long time. She stayed by my side until the paramedics arrived a few minutes later.

The next thing I remember was being wheeled on a gurney out of my house toward the ambulance when the seizure stopped. My right arm felt weak and strange, but I was able to move it. Years later, I was informed by my neurologist I had postictal hemiparesis (Todd's paralysis), which is a brief period of temporary paralysis often following a seizure. When I had Todd's paralysis, I had a brief period of temporary paralysis in my right arm and hand.

According to my neurologist, if I continued to have grand mal seizures, Todd's paralysis phenomenon would get worse each time. I could, eventually, be permanently paralyzed on my right-side extremities. If I had known that before I had a seizure, I would have been more worried. I hoped my seizure was the last one I would have to deal with because of the intense pain and the potentially extreme detrimental aftereffects.

My family followed the ambulance to the closest hospital to give me support. I stayed there for hours until the ER doctor released me. My mother thought I could die the whole time because of the severity of the seizure. She quickly told my neurologist about what happened to me. She was concerned about whether the seizure would become more intense. He emphasized the importance of taking my medication.

I decided my mother was not reliable for giving me my anti-seizure medicine dosages. I began taking it myself. I never again missed a dose since that morning of my first seizure. I learned quickly to take my medicine on time each day. I had my medicine with me if I left my home, for a minimum of twelve hours. Nothing like a ten-minute, violent seizure—along with a doctor warning that if it happened again, you could be paralyzed—to scare you into being vigilant about your medication.

CHAPTER 9

Higher Challenges

Later in the summer, I received a letter about joining the military, and I was convinced that should be my future, instead of higher education. I wanted to serve my country like my grandfathers did, even though I had an injury. My mother called the local military headquarters to find out more about joining. They said I could not participate because I was disabled.

I was crushed because I did not like being called disabled at that moment in time. In my view, disabled meant a person who gave up on recovering from their injury. I was not giving up on my recovery. I had to focus on something else because I would succeed in my professional career. I switched my focus back to higher education.

I decided to attend Waubonsee Community College to get my associate's degree and began to exercise for my recovery in their fitness center. My primary goal was to graduate from a university with a bachelor's degree in education and be in great shape physically. I wanted to save money by taking a lot of the introductory courses at the community college. I would prove to the military and any other nonbelievers I could do anything ordinary people could do. Nothing would stand in the way of my decision to study hard, pass each course, and improve my physical recovery at the fitness center.

Eager to follow in much of my family's path, I decided to get an education degree. Most of my family had graduated with a bachelor's degree and succeeded in their professional careers as educators. My father was successful in teaching United States history, and my mother in teaching English. I would show them and the world I would have a great professional career in teaching.

I needed a tutor and accommodations to get through Waubonsee and move on to a university. The director of Waubonsee disability services said I needed to take an intelligence quotient (IQ) test from a psychologist, hired at the Division of Rehabilitation Services (DRS). My IQ test was to see how much my injury damaged my short-term memory. This would help to determine if I needed accommodations at college and to what degree.

My IQ test was very hard, and I scored a low average of eighty-four points. I was upset because I scored a 110 from the Center, before my surgery, by their psychologist. Ninety to 110 is considered average. I swore I would work to improve my cognitive functions over the next few years at Waubonsee. To pass my courses would be an enormous climb for me in my academics, but my determination, hard work, and willpower to study would prevail.

When I had a meeting with the disability director, Iris, she looked at my medical, psychological, and academic assessment review. She was able to recommend I should have reasonable accommodations. She assigned me a tutor and extended time in taking exams in my courses. I had plenty of time to get my thoughts into answers to pass all my exams.

I believe without those reasonable accommodations, I would have failed most of my courses because of my short-term memory damage. Iris taught me academic and ethical principles so that I would thrive. She cared about me and my potential for a future professional career. She did not give up on me in my academics. Without her help, I believe I would not have been as refined as I was when I graduated from Waubonsee.

In the beginning years at Waubonsee, I thought Iris was mean to me. I kept telling her, many times, I should get more accommodations than she gave me. She scolded me for asking my professors to let me take special exams with open books, which were not approved by the Individuals with Disability Education Act (IDEA) for me.

I got to use the IDEA program because of my learning disability. Federal law required the disability office to serve my educational needs. Not every student with learning disabilities meets the criteria for special education services under the IDEA though.

One time, my health course professor let me have an open-book exam when other students did not because of my learning disability. When I was taking the exam in the disability office meeting room, alone, I saw Iris looking in through the inside window. I could hear her having a conversation with a coworker about my open-book exam. I thought she was talking about how I should not be allowed to have an open-book exam. She wanted me to have accommodations but not have it too easy. I felt horrible during the test time because I wanted her to be proud of what I could accomplish.

Over time, I discovered why Iris was disappointed in me. She wanted me to earn my grades and not be sluggish in taking shortcuts in my courses. She wanted me to be prepared to use what I learned at Waubonsee in the real world so that I would prosper. She wanted me to be successful in my professional career.

My academic instabilities faded away at Waubonsee because I took fewer courses than regular students, which led to me being able to focus and succeed in those courses. My tutors gave me more advice and confidence to succeed in my studies, so long as I worked hard at doing all of my assignments. I did have withdrawals with some of the tougher courses, but it guided me as to what I could do and what I could not do when I decided to pick a major degree program at a university. I was not sure education was what my future profession would be.

Halfway through getting my associate's degree, I decided to switch from education to political science as my major. I wanted to be a role model, advocate, and lobbyist for the disabled. I believed not all people with disabilities felt they had the ability and skills to get a successful professional career. I wanted new laws and programs in the legislative arena for disabled people, so their rights would be protected. No one would be put aside because of their incapacity.

A political science degree would provide me with the ability to experience interacting with different populations, research, oral and written communication skills, and excellent leadership skills. Later in life, I would use my political science degree to get a legislative researching services job in my future professional career. I studied hard so that I could be an example to the students with learning disabilities and the world.

I decided to try to attend Illinois State University (ISU) because they have an excellent disability services department and it was not too far from my hometown. I applied in the fall of my third year, 1999, for the spring 2000 admission, but I was still missing some required coursework to graduate from Waubonsee. I was rejected. When I got my required courses in the spring semester of 2000, I reapplied. Now, I was too late for the fall semester of 2000 admission. I missed the deadline for enrollment.

I exhibited my strong will and ever-increasing confidence by arranging a meeting with the formal president of Waubonsee. He went to the same university I was trying to attend to get his higher educational administration doctorate degree. I must have made a good impression on him in our meeting. He went to bat for me. I was admitted to ISU for the fall semester in 2000. I believe the president was proud of my efforts to graduate from Waubonsee, despite my learning disability. He knew I had received several scholarships, including his scholarship (the President's Scholarship), my last year there. He enabled me to start a better future.

It also didn't hurt that the president knew my father. My father was remotely friends with the president when they both attended college. They bonded when the president was the referee for my father's match for the Big Ten Conference Wrestling Championship. He was proud of my father because he won. The lesson I took away from this was how important it was to never forget people who helped you get to where you are.

In May 2000, I received my associate's degree and gained more confidence. I had achieved another one of my goals. If I had not received my associate's degree, I would have been devastated and unable to prove my hard work to anyone who gave up on me in my high school. I would have been in a deep depression for a long time because I may have stopped believing I could get a great professional job and succeed in the future.

Throughout my time at Waubonsee, my high school friends faded away. However, I did have one close friend left, Tom. In the summer of 1996, after graduating high school, he and I went to a gym to work out together consistently for a few months. I got in the routine of hitting the gym with him like I used to before my injury. He gave me confidence I could lift weights even if gym members looked at me because of my awkward dumbbell lifting style.

Because of Tom, when I enrolled at Waubonsee, I decided to go to its fitness center. It was different from the weight room Tom and I had lifted in. I did not know any of the gym members or staff. I did not care what people thought of me. One of my recovery goals was to continue my recovery exercises by myself and be in excellent shape. I did not want to be at home sitting on a couch watching television or doing other lazy things and not recovering.

My senior year of high school, I was uncomfortable looking at all my friends lifting weights and getting stronger in the weight room. I was embarrassed as I struggled to lift weights. I was worried that when they saw me, they might give up on me.

The fitness center had all of the therapy exercise

equipment I used for my workout at Marianjoy. They had treadmills, ellipticals, free and machine weights, and an area for stretching. They had personal trainers to help new members use all the equipment they had. They could give encouragement to existing members who wanted to get more healthy and fit. I did not use them because I already knew every weightlifting technique for getting into great shape.

Going to the fitness center was my most significant "course" at Waubonsee. I went five days a week to make myself healthy again. I was gaining strength and endurance and burning more fat exercising. I kept weighing myself, before and right after I did my workouts, to see if I needed to gain or lose weight. I reached my weight goal of 170 pounds.

On the first day, I was walking by the weight exercises and saw the barbell bench press. I was nervous, so I did not try to lift any weights on it. I decided to do the bench press machine and dumbbells to gain muscle strength. I knew if I did it for a few months, I would be able to do the barbell bench press.

I improved my physical form by using dumbbells to gain more strength and balance in my upper right extremities. I kept the same amount of weight on both sides of my upper body. I felt awkward when I did dumbbells in the beginning, because other members did specific techniques I could not do at that time. When I did dumbbell bicep curls with my right arm, it was coming up incorrectly and slowly, unlike my left arm. When I got tired during a dumbbell exercise, my right arm gave way ahead of my left arm.

I needed to compromise with my two arms by lifting at the same time. If I got tired and was unable to finish the exercise with my right arm, I would not go ahead with my left arm to get done. I made my arm muscles equal on both sides. I wanted my right-sided extremities to recover more and improve my muscle tone so female students would be interested in my body. I believed they would say yes to a date with me, over time, if I asked them out.

I used the heartbeat program on the elliptical to keep control of my blood pressure and stress so I wouldn't have another stroke, injury, or sickness. If I did, my family would be overcome with grief again because of their worries from my past medical conditions. I improved my balance and mobility by not using the side rails for support on the treadmill when I walked faster. The treadmill has many health benefits, including an increase in the strength of the heart, weight loss, and decreased insulin resistance. Walking or running was a great recovery exercise, and the treadmill put less stress on my body than an outdoor surface. I felt more prepared for my day after my morning workout.

I had trouble jogging on the treadmill in the beginning. The treadmill is a little trickier for me than running on a track. When I began to jog, I succeeded for a few strides, but in about five seconds, I stumbled and fell hard on the treadmill. I did not give up on jogging even though I was nervous and scared. I was worried I might fall off and hurt myself again jogging. My right foot hit the ground too late on my paces because I had weak right quadriceps and foot drop. I got my right foot and quadricep muscles stronger over time as I went to the fitness center.

I wanted to look like the rest of the members who were jogging and get more confidence while doing so. When I failed at jogging, I felt humiliated when I looked up and some members were looking down at me. I did not worry because I knew I would be able to jog. I jogged outside on the grass because it was soft on my feet, compared to pavement. Plus, if I fell, it would not hurt as much. This was a great way for me to improve my running skills so that I could tackle the treadmill again in the future.

My senior year in high school, when I was on the baseball team, I stumbled a lot jogging on grass. I did not have the strength in my right quadriceps. In the weeks following my accident on the treadmill at Waubonsee, I could jog on the grass, and I did not stumble. I built the muscles on my right quadriceps by working out. Eventually, I could jog for miles on the grass.

When I got on the treadmill for the second time, a few weeks later, I was able to jog and did not trip. I kept using the treadmill, and eventually, in a year, I did not limp when I was walking in the cold and in sensitive situations with people. If someone came up to me on the street, I was confident they would not know I had a lasting injury when I walked. Part of what I wanted to accomplish was to renew my ability to fit in. Fitting in had always been important to me. That's why I cherished the fact that I was popular in high school. My injury effectively made me stand out wherever I went. I was different when I wanted to blend in. I'm not sure where that deep desire to fit in comes from. Perhaps it's a bit of insecurity, or perhaps it's just because we all want to belong to someone and something.

One thing I did not do was make friends with members at the fitness center. It was not because I was nervous about my injury. I had improved my confidence physically and emotionally at Waubonsee. Right now, I was in the fitness center for one reason. That was to continue with my physical recovery. However, I eventually would make many gym friends later on in life.

My most significant and essential friend was my brother, who I spent time with when he was attending Knox. My brother and his friends were popular at his college, and they embraced me as one of their own when I visited. They did not view me as a person with an injury but as a person who had a caring heart and a positive attitude. I got more confident through conversations with them and took their advice about getting a date with female students.

One time I went down to see them at his college. We drove from there to Cedar Rapids, Iowa. It was about a two-hour drive. We went to a Kiss concert. It was a packed house. I was very excited. This was the first concert I had ever been to. Kiss used a lot of pyrotechnics. The show did not disappoint. I was happy they had invited me to come along.

I struggled to have conversations with girls at Waubonsee. I was nervous with them. I could introduce myself, but after a few seconds, our conversation would end. I could not think of subjects to talk about at that time. Sometimes, I struggled to comprehend when they answered my questions because I could not listen intently due to my aphasia. A few female students on campus giggled at me, which made me feel I was a failure while talking to them.

One time, I had a chance to have a great conversation with a beautiful female student after a funny, short speech I gave in biology. After class was over, she tried talking to me while we were walking in the hallway to leave the building. Our conversation lasted less than fifteen seconds. I did not have time to think about questions I was going to ask her. I wanted to talk to her, but all that came out was "Hi." She basically just said hi back, and the opportunity was gone.

I believe she thought I was hilarious and cute because of

my speech presentation. I wanted a long conversation with her, but I was nervous. I should have given her compliments so she would know I was interested in her. If we could have had a good conversation, the next time I saw her, I could have asked her out on a date. Maybe it could have blossomed into a relationship.

I needed more confidence with my speech and cognitive ability so I could have conversations with female students successfully and get a date with them. I kept having sessions with Scott, my neuropsychologist, when I attended Waubonsee. Most of my sessions with him helped me get more confidence and self-esteem back when I was talking to female students I liked after my injury.

I became more and more positive over time when I was talking to female students. I knew I could have a conversation with them about my recovery story. Some of them would respect me for telling them, and they might give me empathy. I would find the female student who did not look at me with pity but as a person who was sweet and caring toward her and other people.

My speech ability was improving more than I thought when I graduated from Waubonsee. My mumble stopped when I was nervous because I was practicing more conversations with my family, students, and faculty. I learned different subjects to talk about and listened intently to understand their answers. I asked them more questions. What high school did you go to? What courses and career do you want to be your focus?

One event opened my eyes—when a former close friend disengaged from having a conversation with me. Mike had been my childhood friend through high school. When I saw him in a parking lot at Waubonsee, I believed he was hiding in his car to avoid me. I looked at him with a smirk, instead of ignoring him. I stood by my car and watched him until he pulled away in his snazzy car. I believed if he would have stayed and had a conversation with me, he would have been in awe at my verbal ability. My confidence was growing, and his attitude would not bring me down. Only for a few seconds did I feel hatred toward him. Suddenly, I did not care because I knew I would make new friends.

Once I graduated from Waubonsee, I went back to visit Marianjoy Outpatient Hospital by myself to show my old therapists I was in great shape. They were in awe that I had accomplished many recovery goals I had set with them. They noticed my body, speech, and cognitive abilities were great, compared to what I was like at Marianjoy. They were impressed I was going to attend Illinois State University to further my academic career.

CHAPTER 10

A Time of Leisure and Work

In the summer of 1996, after my high school graduation party, I got a job at a local golf course in Oswego. I learned to be on time, work hard, and save money for college and retirement. A bonus at my job was receiving free rounds of golf so I could improve myself. I figured this would help me beat other golfers in a match.

My golf game was terrible, but I improved with the help of a professional golfer, at no cost to me. He was friends with my father, who was a former athletic director at my high school. Their friendship began when they used to set up schedules for golf events together. The professional golfer did not judge me at my golf game, which suffered because of my right hand. Thanks to his lessons, my right hand did not get in the way of my golf swing, and I could beat most of my family and friends in a game today.

I asked my father if he would like to go on a golf vacation with me, so I could show off my skills before school began in the fall semester, my second year at Waubonsee. My father said yes and was excited to go with me. We decided to go to the Rocky Mountains and check on the land lot we owned in Fairplay, Colorado.

My father and I loved the Rocky Mountains because they were beautiful, and we loved to fish and eat the bass, which was to die for. We went golfing, enjoyed scenic driving routes, and explored many historic towns to see the cultures and monuments. At our hotel, I talked to strangers in the hot tub, and they did not make me nervous because I was improving my conversations.

One of our scenic routes was the Black Canyon of the Gunnison National Park in western Colorado. As we were going through the route, we were right next to a cliff. The cliff was a deep, steep-walled gorge about half a mile long. I was very nervous and scared because if my father drove just a little bit off the road, we would fall to our death. We made it through the scenic route, but I was rattled. I swore I would not go on that route again in my life.

My father and I were coming home, and we stopped in a hotel just outside Denver, Colorado. We watched the weather on the news and were shocked the Chicago area was getting a tremendous amount of rain. We were very concerned about our house being flooded because we live right next to the Fox River. My father called home, but no one answered. I was distraught because my baseball cards were in my desk drawer in my bedroom, on the first floor of our house. I loved my card collection.

Of course, we didn't know it at the time, but that night, my mother was panicking because the river was over the brick patio in the backyard. She called my cousins' house in our town to get my brother. He was house-sitting at that time, but the phone lines were down. My mother left our home to get him, but she was almost swept away in her car by a flooded creek. She gave up on getting my brother and drove back to our flooded home. She did not try to get inside the front door because of the rising water around our house. One of our windows on the first floor was not locked. She opened it to let our dog, Biscuit, jump out of our house.

While my mother was outside our home, she saw one of my friends, who had come down to see if the Fox River was flooding. My mother explained she could not gain access to the house, so he invited her to spend the night at their family's rental home. It was walking distance from our house. The next morning, she saw the damage to our home and was worried about the cost of repairs.

That morning, my father and I hauled ass back home because we still weren't able to get a hold of my mother or brother. When we arrived, we could see the flooded river receding from our house. We were relieved my mother was okay but also worried about the damages. In a few days, my parents found out the cost of repairs to our home from the water damage contractor. We were distraught because the price was high and they did not have flood insurance. I began to wonder if our family was cursed for some reason. Yes, I know, it's irrational to think about such things, but wouldn't you start to wonder?

A year later, in 1997, we still did not have carpet on the first floor because my mother was nervous our house might flood again. I came up with the idea I should sue the hospital for my misdiagnosis by their doctors. I wanted to get money so my parents would be relieved from the cost of repairs.

I asked Scott, my neuropsychologist, for advice, saying, "If you were us, would you file a medical lawsuit against a big medical center?"

Scott said a medical lawsuit could pull a family apart. Opposing lawyers would research everyone in your family and find something we did and did not want anyone to find out about us. They would use that against us so that they could win the medical case.

My mother and I listened to his advice, but we decided to see if I had a suit, to ease our suffering over the years of my recovery. We went to the best law firm in the Chicagoland area, recommended by Scott. I was eager to talk with the lawyers because I was convinced my lawsuit would be a slam dunk.

Our attorneys listened to my medical case about the mishandling of my diagnosis by my former doctors at the hospital. They said I had an excellent medical claim for a lawsuit, but they thought it was not convincing enough for jurors to find in my favor and award me monetary damages. The jurors would get confused with my misdiagnosis and specific details in my case because I went to four hospitals and medical centers for MRIs. The jurors would see me healthy and my improved verbal and physical abilities after my injury.

I would not sue my neurosurgeon at the Center because he saved my life. I idolized him beyond belief. I would have been a millionaire and had plenty of money to spend if I won the medical case. My parents would not have to worry about their finances. But isn't life always like that? The would've, should've, and all that sort of stuff? We can always look back after we've made our choices. We can always play Monday-morning quarterback. The hardest thing in life is to make the right decision at the right time, without the benefit of twenty-twenty hindsight. Very few of us are solid enough at the helms of our lives to make the right tactical moves all the time. Indeed, I don't think any of us are capable of predicting the future. We can only take the best steps we can to make whatever future awaits us as good as possible.

In winter 1998, after my fall semester was finished, I went on my second vacation after my injury, to snow ski in a resort in Steamboat Springs, Colorado, with my uncle Johnny. I wanted to have fun and relax away from my studies. He owned a condominium, so I got to stay for free. I only spent money for travel and food. I felt excited and more independent because my parents were not there to protect me. I could defend myself because I was an adult. I felt most people my age would leave their parents to go on with their life and be free. Truth be told, I had begun to wonder about what was going to happen to me in the future. Would I be able to truly live independently? Would I be beholden to others, dependent on others, a burden on others ... for the rest of my days? The thoughts, oh, those so desolate thoughts, nudged and nagged at me when I let them. I usually was able to shoo them away but not always.

Before my injury, I knew how to snow ski, but now I was horrible because of my injury. I could keep my balance, but I was scared and nervous because I could fall and hit my head. I purchased time with a personal skiing instructor, Barbara, to help me become a great skier. Acquiring Barbara was not expensive if you were disabled or handicapped. She went skiing with me every day I was there, and we became tight friends. She got to know me well. I was slow moving my skies the first morning because of my fear of hurting myself.

I became more confident going down the beginner's hill in the afternoon with Barbara.

On the second day, she convinced me to go down the medium-skill slopes, but I was nervous again. The ski slope was faster than I thought, but in a few days, I got used to the speed, and Barbara was leading me. In a week, I was passing skiers and going down the mountain safely without hurting myself.

After about a week, Johnny wanted me to ski with him and my cousin, Mike, who lived in the Denver, Colorado, area. I felt great my cousin, the sportswriter, came to visit us because he was one of my idols. Mike was excited we invited him because he had never skied with Johnny and me before. We had fun together, but our last time coming down the mountain, I had a grand mal seizure for the second time in my life.

I was happy to be hanging out with Mike on the slopes. I was showing them all of my moves I had learned from Barbara. I was making little cuts to go down a narrow, scenic pathway. When skiing, one must make quick decisions. Due to my aphasia, I was unable to think as quickly as I needed to. I was traveling too fast, and a turn came up on me quickly, and unfortunately, I missed it. I hit the mountainside in such a way that I was knocked backward, with my head smacking against the hard, icy ground. I had a ski helmet on, but the impact of my accident was harrowing, and I was woozy. Johnny and Mike came to my aid, but I said I was fine and got up after a minute. I thought I might have a concussion, but I did not want to tell them because I didn't want to worry them unnecessarily.

I went down the narrow ski pathway again about one hundred yards. Then suddenly I stopped skiing because my legs began to shake. Johnny came to my aid again, and suddenly I fell backward into his arms because I was losing my body control. My legs were shaking uncontrollably. Johnny put me down on my back gently, but my knees were hurting because of the boot binding that locks your foot to the ski. They were in an awkward position. My seizure began, and it was just like my seizure I had once I graduated from high school. It was painful beyond belief.

Johnny had not informed Mike about my level of recovery and need for fluids so I could control my seizures. It was important for me to have a lot of fluids, in my condition, to prevent seizures. I did not have enough fluids in the morning right before my seizure started. My mother told Johnny to make sure I had a lot of fluids at all times on my vacation with him. When my seizure started, Mike was scared because he had never seen one before. He did not know what to do and was relieved when Johnny took control of my situation. Johnny knew what to do and was calm and collected. He learned from my mother's advice.

Johnny told Mike to go down the hill to get help immediately. Mike listened and was skiing fast to get to the emergency telephone. He was not worried about himself. He needed to get the ski patrol to save me quickly.

The emergency ski patrol team came to my rescue within minutes while I was still having my seizure. They carefully put me on their emergency sled and put restraints on me, so I would not fall off into the snow-packed slopes. It took about five minutes until I was at the base of the mountain. By then, my pain was less than when we left the scene of the slope. I was transferred by an ambulance, which was waiting for me when we got to the base of the mountain, to Yampa Valley Medical Center to get examined by an ER doctor.

When I was traveling in the ambulance, my seizure ended, and I did not have any more pain. I was distraught because I could not move my right arm. I thought I had another massive stroke, but I could move my right leg and talk to the paramedics. When I was in the ER, I had to wait about ten minutes until the doctor came. In that time, I was able to move my right arm again like usual. I then assumed my right arm was an ongoing effect of the seizure, so I did not tell the ER doctor or my neurologist what happened. I would learn, much later, this was a symptom of Todd's paralysis phenomenon, just like with my first grand mal seizure.

My ER doctor asked me questions about my seizure to assess my thinking, judgment, and memory to see if I had any mental abnormalities. He examined me by checking my reflexes, muscle tone, muscle strength, sensory function, and motor symptoms to rule out any physical abnormalities. He said nothing was wrong with me. I was relieved he did not say I had a stroke, because I did not want to go through another long recovery.

After my seizure happened, I felt Johnny and Mike would not want to ski with me again. They would have to look after me for seizure symptoms every second. They would think I could not be independent and look after myself and would have to make sure I had enough water, food, and rest.

I would be sure to keep track of my essentials from then on but wasn't sure I would be able to convince them. Later, I would find out that was all in my head. While they both worried about me, they also still enjoyed my company. In fact, I did go on another ski trip with Johnny the following year.

When my parents found out what happened, they were shocked and worried because they felt it could make me regress and become discouraged in my recovery exercises. They were upset at Johnny because he was instructed to be sure I drank a lot of water that day, and he did not follow through. My parents were not mad at me because they knew I had short-term memory damage, but I should have known myself. I was not a baby. My neurologist emphasized the importance of having a lot of water to keep me from being dehydrated, because it could make me have a seizure. I did not blame Johnny but rather myself.

One remarkable thing happened in my recovery on my vacation at the resort. One morning, a few days after my seizure, I was getting up from Johnny's couch where I slept, and I noticed my whole right hand opened up after years of being partially paralyzed. I could not make my fingers open and close independently yet, and my hand was usually partially closed. It was a sign of my ongoing recovery.

The high altitude in the Rockies made it easier to open my hand, according to my neurologist. I called my parents to tell them about my surprising right-hand opening, and they were thrilled for me. They knew I wanted to keep getting more therapy to recover, no matter the cost and time involved. I was thrilled my family had health insurance because my recovery would have been hundreds of thousands of dollars at this point.

When I returned home from my ski trip, I went to Rehabilitation Institute of Chicago (RIC) for more therapy. I believed there would be an occupational therapist there who could improve my right fingers more. I was determined to shake people's hands with my right hand. I would show my family and friends. I would not give up on my recovery, even though my surgery had been three years ago, in 1995.

My primary treatment was injections of botulinum toxin

(Botox) to my right forearm and hand to get more movement in my right fingers. Botox toxin was a lethal poison, but it has been made into a drastic new treatment that could help stroke victims. High doses of Botox could kill patients by paralyzing their body's muscles. Scientists discovered that injecting minute quantities of the poison can help stroke victims regain movement and control. Botox injections were a temporary treatment.

My right hand became loose, and I could pick up easy-to-handle items because of Botox. I had my injections given to me every three months, four times that year. My therapist did not want to overdose me because it could cause more health problems. Each time I received Botox, I was excited because I knew it was working. I was gaining more confidence in shaking the hands of family, friends, and people I just met.

In the early part of my therapies at the institute, my mother would come to escort me and protect me from strangers in downtown Chicago. One time, we took the train to Chicago's Union Station. We both had to use the restroom before we left for RIC. I was done in a few minutes. My mother was taking a long time. Ten minutes had gone by, and I was wondering if she was waiting for me at the main doors. I went to see if she was there. She was not. I came back to the restrooms, and she was still not there. I was somewhat worried, but I waited outside the restrooms. Another ten minutes went by, and she had not come out. I was worried. Finally, my mother came—but not from the restroom.

She was panicked from looking for me in the station. She scolded me for not staying there. I was upset at her because I wanted more freedom. I told her she needed to let me go alone to RIC because she would not always be there to protect me. I had already gone to RIC twice with her on the train and cab. I had demonstrated excellent awareness of directions and landmarks. I promised her I would avoid strangers and be cautious with my surroundings.

My parents approved because they recognized I needed to strengthen my self-confidence, and they knew how serious I was about taking responsibility for myself. From kindergarten on, I showed an ability to think things out ahead of time and stick to a plan. My injury had not changed that. My parents felt cautious, but they also knew I needed to grow.

From then on, I traveled alone to RIC for Botox. I proved to my parents they could trust me with doing more advanced things. I believe it was because of this faith in me, while I was at Waubonsee and RIC, that they agreed to let me go to ISU.

In the summer of 2000, before I left for the university, I was seen by a second neurologist at the Center, who eventually was the director of the Epilepsy Center, professor in the Department of Neurological Sciences, and senior attending neurologist. My neurologist was the best in the country I could find for my epilepsy diagnosis. He was proud I became his patient because of my willingness to keep exercising in my ongoing recovery. I wish he had been my neurologist before I had surgery. I believe he would have convinced me to have surgery earlier than I did, which may have prevented the complications leading to my injury. Of course, that's probably not true. I was in denial. I didn't want to think about brain surgery at the time, no matter how dire the predictions were if I waited. All I wanted to do was fit in with my friends in high school and play sports. In short, normalcy is what I craved, and what I got was the complete opposite.

CHAPTER 11

Illinois State University

I was excited about leaving my parents' house to go to ISU for the fall semester in 2000. I was becoming increasingly independent. I checked in at Atkins Hall, the dorm, at my campus and settled in. Over a couple of days, I met a few students in my dorm who would turn out to be great friends throughout college. I was excited for the fall semester to begin because I would make my parents' proud. I would try very hard to reach my academic goals and graduate.

My first day of the fall semester, I had a meeting with my counselor from disability services. They provided me with a welcoming atmosphere by assisting me within the university community. Just like at Waubonsee, they offered me equal access and opportunity for accomplishing educational, professional, and personal goals and approved accommodation services so I could pass courses and succeed in graduating.

While studying at Waubonsee, I learned from my mistakes in comprehension-course materials. I told my counselor the best way I learned was to have an assigned classmate take notes for me. It was difficult to understand the professors quickly enough to put it on paper. I got to compare his notes and my notes in each of my courses. I used their notes in doing assignments and studying for exams.

If I failed my courses, my parents would consider bringing me back home to attend a local college. I did not want that to happen because I would lose my independence. The cost of living in the dorm was expensive, so my parents would not need much encouragement to have me move back home.

My political science readings, assignments, and exams were more robust than Waubonsee's courses. I spent a lot of time with my tutor, so I would study more to pass each class. The work was too much because of its content and the number of hours required. After a year of taking courses, I met with my political science advisor, and we decided I would switch my major to a minor degree. My stress level was taking away my physical rest and could cause me to have a seizure.

I decided my major degree would be communication studies. I would practice with verbal and writing skills recovery, content, and spent less time studying so I could relax with no stress. Hopefully, this would reduce my stress. When I told my mother, she was surprised because I would have trouble with public speaking. She was worried I would be too nervous giving speeches to professors and students.

I learned from my courses at Waubonsee that speeches were a great exercise for my ongoing recovery. I had to keep giving them in order to practice socializing with other students and people. I believed communication studies was an excellent way to improve my cognitive and speech abilities in one program. Looking back on it now, it seems like a perfectly natural decision, perfectly normal, especially given the fact that I'm in communications as a professional. But back, then nothing was as it seemed. I felt a little like Don Quixote tilting at his famous windmills with his long, slender lance. Why in the world would a guy who'd temporarily lost his speech and his short-term memory even think he could succeed as a communications specialist? People politely asked me this question, although in a couched sort of way, and I always just shrugged off their doubts and moved forward with my plans to build a rewarding and satisfying life for myself, despite my handicaps and hindrances.

I had more help from my tutor with my writing skills and researching assignments. He made me practice writing note cards and speeches the right way. He made me work on my pronunciation so my professors and classmates would understand what I was saying.

I received help to improve my speech and comprehension from the Department of Communication Sciences and Disorders. A few student speech therapists helped me out as an extracurricular private course. They made me more fluent and understandable when I spoke to audiences by improving my articulation.

In my first session with my student speech therapist, I learned and practiced successfully saying R words. I could not say R words correctly my entire life until then, even before the complications from surgery. All I had to do was get my tongue to go upward and back and practice. That was my main speech therapy goal at my university. I had been embarrassed I could not pronounce Rs throughout my life. The fact that my name is Robert made the problem all the more irksome. "Hey, Wob!" my brother's close friends would tease, and so would many more of his friends. "Oh, Wobby, Wobby … woo!" God, I hated the speech problems I had. Those problems made me stand out in his class of friends. They made it hard to fit in with them. They made it hard to be the me I wanted to be. I was scared my family and friends would make fun of me for getting help with a speech therapist, so I kept it private.

No one knew I could not say Rs in high school before my surgery because I was clever enough to hide it. Think about that for a minute. I had to be on my guard every second to make sure I avoided saying any words with the letter R in them. That took a lot of work. Trust me. It wasn't easy. When I attended college at Waubonsee, I went by my first name, Jonathan. When I told some of my college friends at the university my name was Rob, after I corrected my Rs, they had become too used to Jonathan. I got trapped with Jonathan throughout my time at ISU, but I did not mind.

I made more new friends because of speech therapy success. I began socializing with them and improved asking questions. They encouraged me to go up to beautiful female students and do my best at having a conversation. They helped me heal when some attractive female students would laugh at me once in a while. I still had a little trouble mumbling in very nervous situations.

One time, a few of my friends, Todd and George, and I went to a college bar in Bloomington, which was a few miles from our campus. We listened to an excellent local band, relaxed, and flirted with female students. I ran into a high school friend who was best friends with my ex-girlfriend,

Tracy, from high school, who came to visit me at Marianjoy years ago. She told me about Tracy and how she was doing in her life. She was going to the same university and was graduating at the end of that semester. I had two years until I graduated. I told her friend I was doing better since my injury. If I wanted Tracy back in my life, I knew this would be the last chance I had. I decided I had moved on and went back to hanging with my friends. I was not depressed because some day I would have a relationship with a beautiful woman.

George, Todd, and I hung out together most weekends while we were in college. One time, at George's apartment, we had a small party. I was making a funny, rude comment to one of George's female student friends. She hit me on the head when I was lying on the floor. I got enraged at her, stood up (at which point she stood up), and softly pushed her. I had not been hit on the head after my surgery yet in my life. I felt so disgusted by what I did. Before my injury, I knew not to push or hit a woman. It was my instinct that made me push her. I knew I deserved to be hit in the head. I learned a big lesson not to push women, no matter what the cause.

George introduced me to his fraternity because he wanted me to be part of his circle of friends in the fall of 2001. I socialized more with female students who hung out with them on weekends, and they encouraged me to pledge their fraternity. I said absolutely and that I was looking forward to becoming a frat brother. It was important for me to fit in, to belong to an organization that I could be part of. After all I'd been through, all I wanted was to be normal. I didn't want to have to think about R words, brain bleeds, and seizures. I was simply tired of the entire damned thing, and all I wanted was to have a bit of fun and study enough to graduate with the best grades possible.

I made more friends in my pledge class and went to fun events in the fall. On one occasion, at a bonfire, I introduced myself to a beautiful female student from the sorority. We had a good conversation about our plans after college. She gave me her phone number, and it boosted my confidence and self-esteem. I was nervous talking on the telephone, but I summoned the courage to call her in a couple of days. When I called, she was not at home, and I could have left a message, but I was too nervous. My insecurities kept growing after our encounter. I did not call again. I'm sorry about that now, but I understand why I didn't act. The world is scary enough for us all when we're young and just starting out. Imagine how it feels if you've got problems with your brain.

Our pledge class went on a road trip to watch the Chicago Bulls, and we bonded with one another. While our pledge class was traveling, we drove by a few hospitals, including the Center, and that got me thinking. I had come a long way in my journey with my injury. I felt more confident. I did not care if someone looked down at me because I had a lasting injury, or at least that's what I told myself at the time. We all care about how others perceive us, regardless of whether we tell ourselves that we really don't. With age comes wisdom, though, and I can honestly say that the fitting in is less important to me now than it was back in those days of my youth. How people see me is less important too. I guess it's all in how you function in the world and how you accept your place in the bigger picture.

My confidence and self-esteem were high before the initiation week, near the end of the fall semester. The president of our fraternity called me into their house to talk, presumably about being accepted by them. He told me to bring the fraternity paddle and a unique pin they gave me when I began pledging earlier in the fall. I was excited because I was going to be a member.

I met him in a private meeting in the pool table room in the basement of their fraternity. He told me his frat brothers voted to let me go because of my low grades. I said to him, with my eyes wet, "I worked hard at being accepted by your members, and this is what I get? I gave weekends to try to become good friends with you and your frat brothers. I memorized the words of your frat book (which you had to do). I came to all the fraternity meetings and events in the fall so I would be included with the pledge class." They did not respond. I put the pin and paddle on the table and left.

I was devastated, but I had other friends at the university who would always be there no matter what, even if I could not pass a test to be in a fraternity. I still had my best friend from high school, who I kept in contact with. Tom supported me throughout Waubonsee and while I was at the ISU. Once in a while, I went to visit him at his college, University of Illinois at Champaign/Urbana. He was getting his master's degree in nuclear engineering. He got almost all As in his coursework because of his dedication to his studies. He was my role model and made me want to study more and be successful in my professional career.

After college, Tom invited me to his bachelor party at Lake Michigan. We went out on a fishing boat to catch fish and socialize. I was nervous, but I began conversations with Tom's other friends, and I succeeded because of my willpower and confidence. I made more friends in the process. When Tom had his wedding reception a week later, I was seated with some high school friends. I was very nervous, but my confidence and willpower helped me converse with them, thanks to the support and encouragement Tom had given me.

In the spring of 2002, during my second year at ISU, I became friends with Michelle, a beautiful student in my dorm. I wish I could have had a romantic relationship with her, but in order to do so, I would have had to admit to her that I had a horrible accident years ago. I wasn't confident enough yet to share my story with someone I was romantically interested in. I did not want to tell her because I did not know what she would think of me. She began having a romantic relationship with someone else, and our friendship faded. I needed more confidence so I could get a beautiful woman to be romantically interested in me.

I passed all of my courses at ISU because of my hard work, determination, and the support from my family and friends. I graduated in May 2003, at twenty-five years old, with my bachelor's degree in communication studies and a minor in political science. I got a 2.15 GPA out of a 4.0 scale. It was a C average. I believed if a typical student got the same GPA, they might be depressed, but in my case, I was proud of my success. Indeed, simply graduating was a major milestone moment for me, so I didn't really care if I was cum laude.

While I was studying, I went to ISU's fitness center and another local gym to continue my recovery exercises over the time I was there. I went four to five times a week to work out. I improved all of my exercises and put on some lean muscle. I had more confidence in my attractiveness, but I did not go out of my way to make friends there at the gym. I was too focused on getting better results in my recovery.

My graduation success, making new friends, and getting

better in my physical stature at ISU did not put a halt to my expanding medical files when I began school. Within the first year, I had a kidney stone, the size of a pea, in my ureter. The ureter is a tube that carries urine from the kidney to the urinary bladder. There are two ureters, one attached to each kidney.

Kidney stones are hard deposits made of minerals and salts that form inside the kidneys. My pain, caused by a kidney stone, would build up in intensity as the stone moved through my urinary tract. My symptom was a slight pain in my lower right back.

This began when I was eating pizza in my car outside of my dorm. I thought my pain was from lifting weights too hard because I was working out. My pain went away in a few minutes. When I was sleeping that night, I woke up with agonizing pain in the same spot. I got up from bed to call 911 with a hunched back. When the paramedics came and put me on their gurney, I vomited because of the pain. I spent the night at a local hospital to recuperate and take heavy medicine to ease the pain.

The next day, I went to see a urologist at the hospital, and he said instead of having surgery to remove it I should wait because my kidney stone would come out on its own. I waited for two weeks, with heavy pain medicine to ease the agony, as my kidney stone traveled through my ureter. I told my parents I needed a second opinion on my kidney stone because I had not passed it.

I had an appointment with another urologist at Aurora's local hospital, a city just north of my hometown. He said I needed surgery now to remove my kidney stone, based on x-rays and how long I had been in pain. My parents and I agreed with him. This was the first time I would have surgery since my injury. I was terrified and did not want to go under. I remembered waking up from my coma and not being able to move or communicate. I remembered the confusion and the horror of the realization that I was injured. It took all my strength to do it, but I once again had to put trust in my surgeon.

I knew it wasn't brain surgery, but being in the exam room brought up a lot of bad memories. I still hated needles, and they used the mother of all needles to give me an epidural in my lower back, which turned out wasn't so painful. He removed my kidney stone by going through my urethra. The urethra is a tube that transmits urine from the bladder to the exterior of the body during urination. While I was under, he put a black string up my urethra so I would not get a blood clot. I was happy when I woke up to find that everything had gone according to plan.

A week later, when my urologist removed the black string from my kidney, it was excruciating. My father came into my room right after, and I said boldly to get out for the sake of my privacy. I did not want another kidney stone ever again, so I took my urologist's advice not to have caffeine. I still had dark chocolate, which has a small amount of caffeine!

When college ended, I did not get a job that provided health insurance. I obtained group health insurance throughout my life, thanks to my parents. During my time at ISU, my parents helped pass a law (House Bill 3080 in the Ninety-Second Illinois General Assembly) that helped a person who was mentally or physically handicapped and was a beneficiary of his/her guardian, who was a teacher, obtain group health insurance.

Illinois Teacher Retirement System allows unmarried

children who are disabled to remain on their parent's insurance even if that dependent is employed and over the age of nineteen. In 2003, fewer than one hundred handicapped people were affected in Illinois, including me.

My first interview after I graduated from Illinois State University in the summer of 2003 was at Rehabilitation Institute of Chicago, where I had been a patient, for a vendor position. The purpose of the position was to purchase orders, used as a contractual agreement, to buy goods or services. The vendor position required more experience than most vendor positions in hospitals, organizations, and companies. RIC was a famous institute, and they only purchased the best medical equipment and supplies to help patients.

I told the interviewer my recovery story at the beginning of the interview because I had come so far in my education to apply for a job there. I did not get the vendor position, but I received a callback for the position, which boosted my confidence and self-esteem and gave me interviewing experience. The interviewer said there were other jobs at the institute I could apply for, but at that time, I was picky and did not see any job openings I liked.

My second interview was with a sales company in downtown Chicago, a few weeks later. After my initial meeting, I was called back for a second interview because they were impressed by how I answered questions about my résumé. I was able to go out on the road with a beautiful saleswoman to see what she did to sell their products. When we were driving to businesses, she asked me questions about sales. After a few questions, she dropped me off at a bus stop because I gave her the wrong answers.

I was confused by her questions because of my damaged short-term memory, and I was scared of explaining my story.

When she left, I was upset for a few minutes, but I came to my senses and knew sales was not for me. I needed great communication skills to get customers to listen to me and be convinced my product was worth buying. I needed more speech therapy to boost my ability to explain to others what I was marketing. I thought I was done recovering my verbal skills because my injury had been in 1995, about eight years before.

I decided to be a substitute teacher, temporarily, in local schools in my hometown until the school year was done in 2004. I did not need an interview to get the position because, to be a substitute teacher, all you needed was your bachelor's degree. I had to sign some employee papers and give my college records, so the school district administration knew I graduated from ISU.

Substitute teaching was easy for me because I did not have to teach much. I had to take attendance, give them assignments, and provide hall passes to students if they had a good reason to leave my class. I saved most of my income, so I would be able to move out of my parents' house and get an apartment far away, when I had a great job. I wanted to hide from my bad injury memories by leaving my town. I admit that part of me wanted to run away, to bury my head in the proverbial sand. Yet I think the notion of wanting to put distance between oneself and the bad times isn't all that unusual. People just want peace and serenity. They want love and the companionship of others. They don't want conflict and struggle, yet both seem to show up in life with maddening regularity. Love, sadly, is often in short supply.

I asked my father if he would find me a job in politics because he was friends with a former Illinois state representative and House Minority Leader. They became friends when he spoke in my father's history classes many times. The minority leader's office sent me a legislative internship application to fill out to be considered by the University of Illinois at Springfield (UIS) Political Science Department. A week after I turned in my application, I had an interview with the former research director, Scott, from the legislative research staff. He was a state employee but did not work at the university. If I could get his approval, then the political science department would approve the internship.

The internship was downstate in Springfield, Illinois. If I got the position, I would finally be moving out of my parents' house. I felt excited because I knew I would get the internship. All I had to do was be calm, answer basic questions, and have a great smile at the interview. Scott would notice I would have a positive impact on my future coworkers.

I told Scott about my recovery so he would notice my determination and hard work to succeed in my professional career. I would do my best to get assignments done but told him I needed extra time doing them because my cognitive thinking still did not come easily. I would get lost organizing my work.

Scott asked me what Major League Baseball team I liked, and I thought he was joking, but he meant it. I said the Chicago White Sox, and it was the right answer. I did not notice when I sat down for the interview, but behind me was a picture of Frank Thomas, a famous former White Sox player. Scott was a big-time fan of the White Sox, and he saw them play as much as possible. He asked some other generic interview questions, and I was able to answer them appropriately.

A couple of days later, Scott called me and said I got the legislative internship because I was a fan of the White Sox. We had a good laugh. I was expecting his phone call because he had a smile on his face the whole time during the interview. I believed my smile was a significant impact on his decision. Scott was a kind man and liked to joke around, but he also wanted his work assignments done on time, with excellence, by his staff. I was moving! More on that later.

I learned and liked analyzing legislative budgets, resolutions, and bills. I was a good researcher, but I had trouble analyzing bills about pensions, revenue, and confusing bill drafts. Half the time, I did not know exactly what the legislative bill was about. I had trouble going onto the House floor, to a state representative who sponsored my analyzed bill, to help him explain what it did. A few staff members would help me do my analysis, but I needed more assistance.

The most help I received was with my mother's coworker's son, Matt. His mother worked with my mother at Waubonsee. Matt got his legislative internship a year after mine, and he was great at accounting, pensions, and revenue. He was excellent at analyzing tough legislative bills, but he did not want to analyze his resolutions because it was easy for him. A resolution is similar to a bill but easier to analyze. He gave me some tough resolutions, and to his surprise, I was successful in finding articles to answer questions in the analysis.

Overall, I should have had the Division of Rehabilitation Services help me find answers to my legislative analysis questions, so I would not have to have staffers help me as much as I did. Then I would be able to explain my analysis to my state representatives and show the staff I knew what the legislative bill meant by concentrating on essential answers.

After my legislative internship was finished, at the end of June 2005, ten years after my injury, I met with Scott, my director. I said I wanted to continue to work with him. I liked the atmosphere around the office and the friendships I made with my coworkers. I was hired as a legislative analyst and worked to the best of my ability to help improve Illinois.

One assignment Scott gave me was to welcome my high school boys' basketball team to the governor's mansion. He knew I had graduated from there. The basketball team took second place at the state tournament in the 2008–2009 season. It was the furthest our basketball team ever went in the high school basketball brackets. They were rewarded, by the state representatives, with lunch during the spring session to celebrate their accomplishment.

I was very nervous about going to the celebration because I had to confront the basketball coaches. Except for the varsity head coach, Kevin, they were different coaches from when I went to high school. Kevin, in 2009, was a friend of my brother and knew about my injury but hadn't seen me since before my surgery. I had built up confidence since my injury, but this would be a great test because I would be able to talk to someone who only knew me as I was prior to my injury.

In the main hallway of the governor's mansion, I first said hi to Kevin and shook his hand. He was an alumni of my high school and well known in the community because of his work ethic and accomplishments in his life. He did not know who I was, so I introduced myself.

Kevin had not seen me in over a decade, and I might have looked different to him. I said, "I am going to sit down with your team to represent the state representatives." He didn't seem to recognize me still. After telling him I went to school there and after he realized what my last name was, he at least recognized my name. I talked to the basketball team and the rest of the coaches about their season as the event went on. I passed the test of not being afraid of my high school coaches and players.

A few years later, I was moved to the communications department, where I made more coworker friends because I was funny and social with them. I made good friends with two coworkers, Brandy and Jeff. They were very popular in the area and introduced me to many of their friends.

Brandy was similar to my close high school friends because she was beautiful and cared about me more than the rest of my friends. She did not judge me as a person with a lasting injury but as a person who had a great personality and attitude toward life. She helped me with my romantic relationships by giving me great advice about doing the right things to make women happy. She told me to give up on ex-girlfriends I still cared about because they were not worth my time and effort.

The other coworker, Jeff, made me smile and laugh every day. I loved his kindness, sincerity, and jokes about my love life and education. His jibes and funny insults were one reason why I decided to get my master's degree. I wanted to shut him up.

I wanted to keep learning so my damaged short-term memory would improve more than it had. I wanted to get a better job than I had now so that I would have more spending money. I wanted to show anyone who did not think I could get an advanced degree they were wrong. I wanted my writing to be perfect so I could motivate myself to graduate.

I tried to get into the communication, public

administration, and psychology master's degree program, but I was denied from the colleges in central Illinois. I had less than a 2.5 GPA from my bachelor's degree at ISU, which came back to haunt me. I tried to convince the college advisors by explaining my story, but they still rejected my applications.

I felt hopeless, but the last advisor I had at University of Illinois at Springfield listened to my story and was impressed by how I got to where I was. He would put me into his human services master's degree program, with a concentration on child and family studies. In order to do that, I first had to pass an abnormal psychology course at Lincoln Land Community College in the summer of 2009. If I passed the required course with a C or better, I would be accepted by their facility.

I worked hard at my abnormal psychology course, and I passed with an A or 4.0 GPA. An A was the highest grade possible! I proved I would pass each class with an excellent grade. I learned from my past mistakes, taking multiple courses and getting lower average grades than I wanted. From the fall semester of 2009 on, I took only one class each semester, so that I could focus on that subject. My professors were strict with all of my assignments, but I saw them every week in their office to make sure I was not behind in my work. I was still working in the communication department as I was taking master's courses in my early thirties.

I took advantage of the services from the disability office and student tutors about two to three times a week. I did not get as much tutoring earlier in my college career because I thought I could do my assignments with less help. The tutors helped me by explaining my assignment instructions and guided me to prepare projects and speeches. They gave me confidence I could do all of my assignments and earn an excellent grade if I tried hard enough.

I used the learning center to get help from excellent student writing tutors to help correct my difficult papers. They taught me creative writing, word-finding skills, and the definition of words I could not understand. Midway through my courses, my writing improved. When the time came for my final master's capstone research project, I was ready.

The capstone would show I had acquired all the knowledge and skills necessary for a master's degree in my concentration. The capstone required the identification of a critical issue related to my concentration; the development of a case scenario that illustrated the critical issue; a review of the literature that substantiates the critical issue with the best-practice approach to deal with the issue and goals, objectives, and interventions section.

My capstone paper topic was "The Impact of a Teen's Traumatic Brain Injury on Depression." I picked this topic because I understood people who had a traumatic brain injury. A traumatic brain injury is brain dysfunction caused by an outside force, usually a violent blow to the head. Traumatic brain injuries often occur as a result of a severe sports injury or car accident. My injury did not qualify as traumatic because it was not caused by an outside force. I understood people who had this kind of injury because of what I had been through. I had overcome my depression from my injury through counseling and encouragement from family and friends to reach my recovery goals. My presentation was a home run with my professors. I graduated in 2014 with a master's in human services. That is an accomplishment no one can ever take away.

CHAPTER 12

New Relationships

In June 2004, at age twenty-six, I moved from my parents' house to Springfield, Illinois, for my legislative analyst internship. I did not know anyone except a lobbyist, Ed, who worked for a big insurance company. He was the brother of my mother's coworker. She said Ed would take great care of me and put me under his wing because he was best friends with Scott, my new boss. He knew many other well-known political people in Springfield and beyond to introduce me to.

I got to stay at Ed's house the first night, and we went out to a famous local pizza restaurant, where I was introduced to a few of his friends. I had a great time because I felt at home with them. I could stay at his house for a while, but I needed to find my apartment fast. I wanted to be independent in my new life and city.

I checked out a few apartments around Springfield

the next day, but they were not the type of atmosphere I wanted. I wanted to find a young adult apartment complex with a swimming pool, because it was the right spot for beautiful women to hang out. I looked at the last apartment on my list, and it was affordable and had a nice outdoor swimming pool and exercise room. I was hooked.

Once I was settled, I was lonely, and I did not go to social events for the rest of the summer because I didn't know anyone very well. I met a young man next door to me, but I did not ask him and his friends if I could tag along with them on weekends. I did not want to be annoying because I was not outgoing enough with people I didn't know. I did not talk to any women in my complex in the beginning because I was nervous. I needed a wingman to give me more confidence, like I had with my friends at college.

When my internship began in the fall, the other interns and I met once a month, at a class, to learn the art of analyzing bills. I started to meet more friends in class. We would hang out on weekends to socialize. I became good friends with one intern, Kareem, who was handsome and African American. We had common interests in interacting with people. I was able to be more confident with him by my side and was less nervous talking to new people.

In the spring of 2005, I made more new friends at my apartment complex. I liked them because they judged me by my character rather than by my injury. They were like my old high school friends because they had similar characteristics and were popular in their social group. We would hang out on weekends at dance clubs, cookouts, and area events. I was not nervous around them, and I found good subjects to talk about to keep our conversations going because we loved sports and women.

I had a great relationship with one of my apartment friends, Scott, because he made me feel more relaxed when we hung out together. We talked more than most of my friends. We loved talking smack about our favorite college football teams. His was Notre Dame University, and mine was Northwestern University. The only thing he did not like about me was when we went golfing. He was a competitor at golf, and I was a goof-off, throwing golf balls in front of him when he was about to tee off.

A year later, one of our friends, Ryan, who lived in the same apartment complex, invited us to his bachelor party at Lake of the Ozarks, Party Cove. He told me there would be plenty of opportunity for a physical relationship with a beautiful woman because there would be many there. I said I would go. I was desperate for an intimate relationship, but I was still nervous about having a conversation with someone I was attracted to.

Our group left early on a Saturday morning in August 2005. When we got in the SUV, I got into the middle of the back seat because they asked me to. I was nice because I wanted to become friends with all of them. After we drove a little while, I complained because of the uncomfortable middle seat. My friends began to giggle. They were used to the guy in the middle complaining and had been expecting it. I was agitated with them that morning.

We traveled about five hours to get to the lake, but I love long traveling adventures. Ryan, who was having the bachelor party, rented a condominium next to the lake from a friend of his. At ten o'clock in the morning, a small boat came to get us to take us to Party Cove. Our group took off our T-shirts, and one person made a funny comment about my body. I was thinking I needed to work out more because

I had little muscles compared to theirs. Most of them were very fit and good-looking.

He made me feel depressed for a moment about my body, but I realized he was not an empathetic person. From then on, I swore I would keep lifting weights and do cardiovascular exercises almost every day to build my body more. I wanted to be like they were, with confidence about their bodies, and swore not to care so much about what people say.

When we got to Party Cove, it was a remote, isolated area on the lake. I expected a large number of partiers would be getting drunk and having a great time in the morning and throughout the day. I was disappointed when we got there because there were only about ten small boats with a few partiers. We arrived on our big boat, and I went up the steps to the balcony to see the scenery. I saw beautiful young women with their tops off right next to our boat. My disappointment went away, and I knew I would like Party Cove.

We sat down for about twenty minutes and listened to music and exchanged jokes. I stood up every few minutes and saw partiers with lots of little boats coming to Party Cove each time. A few hours later, beautiful young women were begging us to let them come on our boat. By the end of the afternoon, most of our group was drunk and flirting. I was buzzing but not drunk because I could not have too much alcohol. If I did get drunk, I could have seizures because of my medication side effects.

I was nervous about flirting, so I did not say much to the women. I could not think of what to ask or say to them to have a good conversation because of my aphasia. I was jealous of most of my group because they were succeeding in making the right moves and inviting them to come out with us that night to bars. We made it back to the condo, and I took a short nap before going out for the night.

Later that night, most of our group flirted with young women at each bar, including me. I was a disappointment to myself because I was nervous at Party Cove. I was determined to succeed in flirting that night. Bars were more entertaining than the Party Cove because I was flirted with and kissed by a few women. They were drunk, but I had more confidence from them coming up and talking to me. I was not picky about which women I had a conversation with because I would not see them again after that night. One of us did have an intimate relationship that night … but it wasn't me.

I noticed when I drank beer, I was less nervous. When I was at Illinois State University, I only had a couple of beers once in a while with my friends, each night on weekends. I did not believe in heavy drinking and was cautious with my medicine. My current neurologist said I could have one, twelve-ounce beer each hour. In college, I did not have any beers when I was talking to young women because I was nervous, thinking about what to say. I did not date a lot at ISU because I feared what they might think about my injury. I was worried about how they would perceive it and not agree to go out with me.

My confidence rose at the lake because I did not care what women thought about me now. I was a caring person, and if a young woman judged me because of my injury, I did not mind. Many women would date me because I was caring and sincere.

From then on, when I went out on weekends to bars and events, I would have a few drinks. I began talking with women I liked to build more confidence. I was able to think of what I would say to them every time I had a conversation because of repetition. Over time, I was a pretty good flirt, like I used to be before my injury.

Once I got home from the Lake of the Ozarks, I wanted a real romantic relationship with a woman. I felt great flirting with women at the lake bars. I decided to go on a dating website. I was timid about finding a relationship online. A woman could be interested in my profile, but they might not be interested once I told them about my injury. My desire to go on a date outweighed my hesitations, and I was up for the challenge.

In the beginning, I did not tell women my story because I feared they might back away from having a relationship. I believed they would not want to get to know me more once I told them. I was not getting anywhere on dates, so I decided I would tell my story after all. If women backed away from me when I told them, I did not want to date them anyway. I was succeeding with my recovery, and if they could not see that, they were the ones with the issue, not me.

Three relationships blossomed out of the dating site, and the women were beautiful, intelligent, funny, and caring. My confidence grew when I told them my story on our first date. They did not shy away from me when I was done talking. They did not mind if I had an injury years ago. They liked my personality and physical looks. It broke the ice between us because they told me some of their problems and issues. We had fun together at wineries, social events, concerts, traveling, and spending time with each other.

My relationships grew beyond belief, mainly because of my confidence and self-esteem. I was attractive to them because of my hard work exercising, excellent fashion style, and taking care of myself. I noticed most women did not judge me by my injury.

The week after the bachelor party, I signed up at a gym to work out and improve my recovery. The gym I started at had much more equipment and options for working out than the small room in my apartment complex. I wanted to show my friends I would get as toned as I could. Before my friend's bachelor party, I had not used the exercise room in my apartment complex because I was too lazy.

I began lifting weights and doing cardio exercises again to build up my muscles and stay in shape. I went four to five times every week for about an hour. I improved my endurance each month. Sometimes I was not enthused about going, but I went anyway because of my determination and willpower. I did not make friends at the gym at that time because I was focused on working out.

In a few years, small gyms began opening up, and they offered low-cost memberships. My gym was expensive, and they had me sign a contract for one year. I left them, after the year was up, for a small gym that did not have membership contracts. I could come for a month and decide to go to another gym without getting charged a fee for leaving.

They had all the equipment I needed to do my recovery exercises. I hoped to recover further at this point because of my ongoing determination to be normal again. I began socializing with gym members, and I told a few of them about my recovery story. Instead of not wanting anything to do with me, they congratulated me for coming to the gym. From then on, I did not shy away from other members because I was more confident.

In 2009, I became great workout friends with Chris because he was strong, healthy, intelligent, funny, and caring. We both enjoyed working out with each other, going to social events, and relaxing from work by having cookouts.

He gave me more confidence in talking to beautiful women and introduced me to his friends, who boosted my self-esteem even more.

When Chris had his bachelor party in 2014, he invited his best friends, including me, to St. Louis, Missouri. I had not yet been to St. Louis, so it was an adventure for me. We watched a Major League Baseball game between the St. Louis Cardinals and Atlanta Braves. He was a huge Cardinals fan and loved going to see them play every season. The Cards won the game! Even though it wasn't my favorite team, I enjoyed going to the game.

We went out that night to bars, where we danced and had a great time. Some of his friends and I flirted with girls throughout the evening. His friends respected me and thought I was funny and cool.

I became great workout friends with another member at the same gym. Tim was older but very intelligent and caring. He welcomed me every time I went into our gym. He and I connected because we both graduated from ISU and we loved to socialize. He introduced me to his friends outside of our gym by inviting me to watch sports together. He made me feel needed in our group because of his stature and popularity.

He and I would always go to ISU homecoming football games, starting in 2017. I thanked Tim and his college friends for inviting me to be there to chill with them at their tailgate party. I met new people every year in the north parking lot of the football stadium. Walking to the stadium, I passed by some fraternities that were having cookouts before and after the game. I wanted to flirt with female students at their parties, but I got the feeling I would get beaten up because I was a stranger and older than they were.

I decided to join LA Fitness, a new gym, because my

former gym did not have enough female members. I wanted to make more friends too. This was one of the biggest gyms in town. There was plenty of equipment for me to choose from to do my exercises. I became good friends with another member, Steve, and his friends, but early on in our relationship, they did not talk to me much. When I told them my story, we connected. They were amazed I had come so far and liked my personality and confidence. They introduced me to their friends, and we got along well.

I looked up to my new friends. They loved to socialize, and they had stature among gym members. They treated me with respect and gave me advice about my physical looks so that I would improve my attractiveness to women. Their support and encouragement made me more determined to succeed in my new life.

Because of my gym friends, I decided to set new goals so I would look great like they did. I wanted to bench two hundred and thirty pounds, so I would match what I was able to bench before my injury. I would get more muscle on my chest to help me look buff. I wanted to work up to eight repetitions of dumbbell curls with thirty-five pounds to get bigger arms. I wanted to do leg presses with six plates weighing forty-five pounds each on each side, by fifteen reps so I would be sure not to stumble when I was jogging. I wanted to run a mile in seven minutes so that I would be in great shape. I did not want to stop going to the gym or detour from my dedication and hard work toward accomplishing my new goals.

In 2007, I needed a great wingman to find a great relationship, and I found more than I bargained for when I met two new friends at my work Christmas party at a nice bar/restaurant.

Eric and Brian were watching me flirt with two beautiful women and making them laugh by playing a drinking game. They were impressed with my determination to try to impress them. They believed most men did not have my courage to go up and chat with new women.

From the first moment I met my friends, I knew they were popular in the area. Their friends admired them, and so did I. I was comfortable talking about things we both had in common, especially beautiful women. They were like my high school friends but older and much wiser because of age and experience. I grew more confident when I became great friends with them.

A few weeks later, Brian had a cookout at his house with a few of his friends and invited me to come. As we were talking, I told them my story about my injury. They were proud of me for what I had gone through, and I did not hide anything from them about my injury.

My friends were trustworthy, reliable, and protective of me. I was building more friendships while hanging out with them because they helped me socialize. They gave me more confidence, and I was becoming popular within my social group.

One weekend, my friends introduced me to two women at an after-hours bar downtown. Cindy and Clarissa were older than me, but we had common interests, and they were popular among our social group. We liked to watch local bands, dance, and socialize. They invited me to go with them to many events every year, to have a great time. They gave me encouragement and great advice about my relationships, despite my speech difficulties. They gave me more confidence to talk to women.

CHAPTER 13

More Confidence

In 2007, twelve years after my injury, I bought a house on the west side of Springfield. I wanted to build up equity in a home rather than give a portion of my income away in my rental apartment payment. My parents were hesitant about giving me some money for the down payment because it was a lot of work to own a home. They were nervous about whether I would be up to the challenge because of my short-term memory damage, but they took a chance, hoping for the best outcome.

I convinced my parents my house would be a great asset and a long-term investment. It would go up in value over time so I could get a more beautiful home in the future. I would get tax breaks from the deductions on my mortgage interest. Owning a house would also provide security to make me feel safe and stable in my community.

Searching for my new house took another six months because I kept changing my mind about what I wanted. In the beginning, I wanted a new duplex with a vaulted ceiling, but I changed my mind dramatically. At the end of searching, I was looking at a small, single-family house that was affordable on my budget. I bought a single home ranch in a nice, older neighborhood close to my work.

With the help of my Realtor and a special program that financially helps disabled people acquire a home, I was able to own my house with little financial help from my parents. I was excited and gained more confidence and self-esteem because I picked where I wanted to live without help from my family or other people. I had a tight budget to go out on weekends with the monthly payments on my mortgage, but I did not mind.

The first day I moved into my new house, my neighbor knocked on my front door. Dave was an elderly man who welcomed me to the neighborhood. Over time, we became good friends, and he strengthened my sense of pride in my home. He gave me security because I could depend on him if I needed something. In return, I went with him to his Baptist church on a weekly basis. I had not gone to church yet, as a weekly routine, in my life, and I was not religious at that time. He brought me to his Bible school class so I would learn their beliefs and faith in God. My confidence grew while being there because members did not judge me for having a lasting injury.

In April 2014, I decided to stop going to Dave's church because my beliefs and values were not the same as his. He told me it was a sin if I was late to church service or drank alcohol. I enjoy drinking socially. I felt awkward with him because I wanted to go alone and pray with no distractions.

I wanted my church to have a great atmosphere and a considerable amount of attendees so I would make more friends.

I decided to go to West Side Christian Church because it was one of the most prominent churches in central Illinois and had much to offer. I joined their church team as a volunteer, greeting people with a great smile as they walked into the church service. My smile puts others in a happy state of mind and makes me more confident in myself. I set a goal to talk to many members, nonmembers, staff, and visitors in order to make more friends and practice my speaking skills.

I joined a support group called Rooted in January 2018 at West Side. My support group gave me the chance to connect with God and use the Bible in ways I never had before. I became involved in improving my faith and beliefs in order to live a deeper and more meaningful life. I got to know Jesus better and accepted life with him. I made friends in our group in the process.

Before joining the support group on Sunday evenings, I was skeptical about what I was getting into because it could be a waste of my time. I could watch National Football League playoffs, March Madness in college basketball, or go to a winery on Sunday instead. When our support group met, we discussed our issues and let our emotions out about our relationships and problems we had. I gathered the willpower to tell them my story and all the questions and concerns I had to overcome.

The support group helped heal me emotionally, unlike anything I had ever experienced in my life. I was a new man by the time we were done meeting, after just a few months, because my group friends gave me more confidence and self-esteem. They reassured me I would live life from here on out with a happy demeanor, despite the obstacles I had to endure. After a few months, we stopped meeting at the church. They still met elsewhere, and I joined them occasionally for a year.

Several years ago, I let my mother know I was attending church and spoke of my intention to continue. I urged her many times to attend church, but she resisted. Soon after our conversation, in 2017, my uncle Johnny, her brother, lost his driver's license, but he badly wanted to continue attending church. Because of his deteriorating condition, my mother agreed to drive him to services on occasion. At the first service, she was overwhelmed. The sermon was based on passages from Isaiah—the same passage she had whispered to me when I was in a coma in 1995. It was being read as part of the priest's sermon. My mother froze, just as she had done years ago, because she was being reminded of the miracle and faith. Since that time, my mother has routinely gone to church on a weekly basis.

In 2015, I ran into a close friend from high school, Leslie, leaving a parking lot in Springfield. She was one of a few students who visited me at the Center right after my surgery. I turned around and pulled up next to her and her daughter. I got out of my car with a big smile because I had not seen her for about a decade. We hugged and talked about our past life adventures.

She was impressed by my recovery. She did not know I'd had a great speech therapist, Gale, to polish my conversations a few years earlier. Gale had helped me to not be nervous by practicing hard-to-say long verbal words almost perfectly.

In the spring of 2016, I was browsing my social media

posts and saw my high school class was having their twentieth reunion on Father's Day weekend at a bar and grill in my hometown. I had not gone to my tenth reunion in 2006 because I did not see the invitation. I was nervous about seeing my friends, and my confidence was not as high as it is today. I decided to go and counted down the days until it arrived. I wanted to demonstrate I was back, with a great attitude toward life.

Meeting my old friends and classmates was a big step toward getting more confidence, but it was also a challenge. I had accomplished a considerable amount of my recovery goals so far, and I convinced myself it would be easy to say hello to my class. My new friends and coworkers encouraged me to go because I would get to demonstrate my hard work in my ongoing recovery.

I texted Leslie to find out if she was going to the reunion. She had been very popular in high school and remained so today, but she said she was unable to attend. She told me I should go to show my high school friends and classmates how far I had come in my recovery.

I also texted my friend and coworker Josh. He was also living from up near my hometown. I mentioned I would be up there for the reunion. He said he would be there that weekend to march in the annual Father's Day Parade, supporting his state representative and our friend Keith, the following Sunday.

The night of the reunion, coincidently, I bumped into Keith. We had a short discussion on politics. He was not there for the reunion but happened to be at the venue because it was near his district. He was one of the politicians I liked chatting with because he was down to earth and not stuck up. Most of my nervousness about talking to my class went away because he made me comfortable.

During our reunion, my classmates and friends saw how much I had improved during my ongoing recovery. I walked normally and gave handshakes to most of them, and my verbal ability was perfect the whole night. I talked to half of my class who showed up, and a few of them wanted more information about how I had come so far in my recovery. I said it was my determination and hard work in all the recovery exercises that made me successful so far, but I was not done yet.

The main classmate I wanted to talk to was another of my close friends. I gave Jessica a longer hug than I usually give to people if I've just met them for the first time. I had not seen her for almost twenty years, and she looked as beautiful as the day I saw her last. She complimented me on how great I was looking and talking, like nothing had ever happened to me. I cared about her opinion because she had not given up on me during my ongoing recovery.

The next day, Father's Day, I had one more thing to do that would make my weekend victorious and give me more confidence. I walked with Josh and many others in the Father's Day parade, supporting Keith. Before the parade, I said hi to one of my brother's friends who was running for a local political position, marching ahead of us with his support group. He knew me through my brother. I shook his hand with my right hand, but he did not seem to know who I was. I told him my name, but he looked at me, dumbfounded.

I believe he was stunned that I had significantly improved. I bet he thought I would have had trouble speaking well enough to have a conversation with him. I believe he was in awe of my recovery, and my confidence grew.

When the parade began, I saw some of my old friends and classmates I had not seen at the reunion. They were on the sides of the streets and waved at me. I felt popular again. I felt like I belonged. I fit in again, and that felt absolutely marvelous.

CHAPTER 14

Health and Recovery

One of the potential pitfalls of my condition is the prospect of losing my marbles down the road because of my stroke. It's a sad reality, but people in my particular slice of the disabled community are more likely candidates for dementia than most others. The idea that I could lose complete control over my mind scared the hell out of me. After all, I'd experienced such a lack of control in the past. I couldn't think, walk, or talk right after my coma. I saw and heard things that weren't there. I literally thought I was going insane, despite the fact that the doctors told me that hallucinations, paralysis, and speech impediments were normal after coming out of a drug-induced coma, and after such a severe brain injury that resulted from the internal carotid artery branch bleed.

To counter this horrific disease, I did many preventative

things. I used the sauna a few times a week at the gym. I had read that, for the male population, average to high regularity of sauna bathing can help reduce risks of dementia. I was also told by many gym members that saunas would help my body cleanse itself, removing toxic fluids so I would not get sick. Additionally, I exercised to stimulate my crucial brain cells to improve my short-term memory. I learned that after I did my whole workout, my stress from my daily assignments at work and from problems with relationships was lower.

I am in great shape because I did not quit my recovery exercises. In 2017, I ran my first 5k. I worked up to jogging that distance. I have run that same 5k each year since then.

Beginning in 2018, I maintained a healthy diet by eating organic blueberries, bananas, corn, whole grains, lettuce, and protein foods every day. I cut down on my calories from saturated fats and sodium. Therefore, my body was refreshed, and I had more energy to do more exercises.

I do not smoke because it doubles a person's risk of getting a stroke and heart disease, and my risk is already higher than the average person. Smoking also causes blood vessels to narrow, which leads to condensed blood delivery to body tissues. It could lead to a severe condition, especially in my case. Smoking increases my risks for weakening and ballooning of my blood vessels, recognized as aneurysms. A rupture of an aneurysm could lead to another stroke or sudden death. Smoking could cause lung disease, weak bones, cancer, immune problems, asthma, and health-care costs.

I am a moderate drinker of alcohol, and I do not use any illegal substances because they can cause cancer, high blood pressure, stroke, and sudden death. I do mental exercises by playing brain games, such as chess, on the internet that keep my brain working every day and help my brain's overall strength in learning.

In 2017, my current neurologist reduced the dosage of my medicines, because of their side effects and my recovery. It had caused unwanted side effects in my health and physical activities. I understood why my neurologist called me intelligent over recent years. I noticed my short-term memory damage had improved, and I became more alert by taking less of the meds. My speech and word finding were faster and easier respectively. My anxiety was less, and I was less fatigued working out.

In July 2018, when I was almost fully off Keppra anti-seizure medicine, my parents had their fiftieth wedding anniversary party and I noticed my right hand was extended fully. The first noticeable movement of my right hand was when I shook my former high school football coach's hand. He was a guest at my parents' party. After that, I went and shook many hands with a fully open right hand. I believed the medicine had been holding me back and preventing my right hand and fingers from improving.

I did not say anything about my right hand and fingers to my family at the time because I was in shock. I had more confidence throughout the party because I was genuinely continuing to recover. I knew in my heart that the use of my right hand and fingers were improving more than I thought was possible.

When the party was about to end, we had speakers to congratulate my parents for getting along and loving each other for fifty years. The lead speaker was my cousin Mike, the same cousin who had gone skiing with me years ago. When he asked me if I wanted to talk, I said yes. I was nervous, but I got up right away and walked to the front stage. I began speaking about my parents, but I did not expect it would be emotional. I had tears in my eyes because my family had gone through so much during my recovery. When I finished, I felt great because I had become less nervous as I continued to speak.

A few days later, I woke up in the morning, and I could move my right fingers individually. I was so happy that I gave my right middle finger to many of my friends to boost my confidence and self-esteem. A month later, I picked up a pen with my right fingers and placed it in my right hand. I wrote a sentence, with a good grip, which I had not been able to do before since my injury. Can you imagine not being able to hold a pen, sign your name the way you used to, and all other such things that come when you've experienced an event like mine? So, the simple bit of progress with the pen was momentous for me, both in terms of practicality and in terms of my emotional outlook for the future.

Monday, the next workday, I showed my coworkers I could write sentences with my right hand. Since that time, I had not been to any therapy to relearn to write with my right hand. I retaught myself to write with my right hand. Before my injury, I was right-handed, but since then, I had become used to writing with my left hand. A few weeks later, I could throw a slightly deflated football with my right hand. When I go up to friends, I give them a great handshake without being nervous. I am proud of what I can do with my right hand today.

In September 2018, I had a yearly appointment with my neurologist, normally a pretty routine checkup, but on this occasion, I was excited to show movement in my right fingers. He was pleasantly surprised because patients with my level of injury usually do not make it this far in their ongoing recovery. Although I had recently been able to fully open my hand and use my fingers, when it was open, my fingers were not all perfectly straight. He recommended I should see a plastic hand surgeon to discuss options for my right middle and ring finger deformity, to see if we could correct it.

I decided to make an appointment with the chair of the division of plastic surgery at Southern Illinois University School of Medicine in Springfield. I was skeptical, trying not to get my hopes up that the surgeon could fix my fingers. To my disbelief, the surgeon said he would fix my finger's tendon. He said I would be able to use it to its full potential, and it would look normal. I came out of our consultation with hope because I was on the right track to a full recovery.

In the early morning on Tuesday, April 16, 2019, I went in for surgery on my right middle and ring fingers. I went to the local medical center early in the morning, nervous because it reminded me of the day of my brain surgery. I knew how risky a general anesthetic could be. Anything could go wrong. I fought back my fear, and the anesthetists knocked me out. After an hour, my surgery was a success. I had a big cast on my right hand when I woke up. One side effect I had from the general anesthetic was I kept saying I wanted to kiss the surgery nurse for a few minutes. She was very cute.

My nurse told me to keep my right hand and arm up as much as I could so my blood would not flow into my right fingers too much. If my right arm was down when I slept, I would be in severe pain. I was released from their care at the center later that morning, a little loopy from the surgery medication. Jeff, from work, gave me a ride home from the local medical center.

I went home to rest for the day, with no pain. I was too stubborn to use the medicine until I went to bed. At three o'clock early Wednesday morning, I woke up from the pain. As minutes went by, it became worse and worse. I took the pain medicine to ease the throbbing, but it took an hour to kick in.

My right hand and arm had fallen from the pillow while I slept. I put a pillow next to me on my right side to hold my right arm up. I made sure my right hand was above the rest of my body to decrease the blood flow into it. It fell off again. I was close to going to the emergency room because of the pain, but I did not.

I raised my right arm to let the blood flow back from my right hand. In about two hours, it worked! My hand pain eventually settled down. To be on the safe side, I did not fall asleep the rest of the morning. Later in the morning, I called my surgeon's nurse and asked if I could have stronger pain medicine. She said yes. As days went by, the pain improved, and my fingers' swelling went down a bit. I could deal with the pain, knowing that, in the end, my fingers would look and work better.

A few weeks later, I was examined by my surgeon to see how much movement I had in those fingers. I moved my right ring and middle fingers properly without deformity. It was an incredible feeling because I had achieved another goal in my life, twenty-four years after my stroke. They say that life is a journey, and that's true. When I was in my teens, before the surgery, it seemed like the world was full of options because my journey was just beginning, and then it took a turn nobody could have predicted. Everyone has a unique path to follow, including me. It's just that the usual milestones you celebrate as you go through life were always overshadowed by the effects of what happened to me on that terrible, life-changing day in the OR. Any progress on the long road back to a normal life was something to cheer.

In July 2019, Brandy, my friend from work, invited me to her cookout once more, and I accepted because I now had a huge amount of confidence and was not nervous to meet all her guests. She had invited me to come to a cookout at her house two times in the past. I did not go because I had been scared about all of her friends who would be there. I worried they might be stuck up and not talk to me because most of them have excellent jobs.

I showed up at her house Friday night. This was the first time my right fingers would do their work in shaking a lot of hands. I went around her nice house to the gathering. Her backyard was beautiful. It had a swimming pool, hot tub, a band, waiter, bartender, beautiful women, all the beer I wanted, and a nice view of the lake in the background. I walked down their gorgeous stone walkway to the cement flooring surrounding the pool. I noticed there were about one hundred guests.

The first person I saw was Brandy, and she gave me a hug. She welcomed me, and we talked about half of a minute. I knew she was saying hi to everyone coming to the cookout, so I cut my talk short. I introduced myself to about fifteen people. My right handshake was awesome. I left Brandy's cookout feeling great. I was not afraid of giving handshakes to people anymore.

In the afternoon of January 21st 2020, I had my right thumb surgery. I was considering not having surgery moments before the nurse came into my waiting surgery room to walk me into the OR. I fought away my fears. After my surgery I had a little pain for a few days. This time I kept my right arm upward at all times. When I returned to my surgeon's office a week later, to get a check-up on how my right thumb was doing, I had more movement!

My positive attitude and intuitive insight into the value of living were what helped me overcome my challenges and fully recover. I learned valuable things about how important my ongoing therapy was for me, because I built more confidence and willpower to succeed in my new life. It is amazing how young human brains recover and prosper after a severe brain injury, over time, if you have the will to exercise daily all parts of your body, mind, and spirit.

I do not want sympathy, because I desire to project peace and happiness within me. I always smile to friends and people I do not even know. I want people to look at my life and be happy because of my successful career, education, and social life. If I had another severe injury and survived, I would not give up on myself. I would focus and thrive on getting better again through therapy.

I am blessed to be alive because of my neurosurgeon's quick actions when he stopped the bleeding during my brain surgery twenty-five years ago. After years of committing myself to recovering as much as I could, I now say I can do anything I want if I put my mind to it. I prospered in my physical, verbal, mental, and emotional abilities because of my determination and hard work and the encouragement of people who did not give up on me.

We all face adversity in our lives. We all have struggles at one point or another. The important thing is to never give up when the going gets tough. The tendency is to seek the path of least resistance, but in doing so, we miss out on important opportunities to become stronger through the hard times. With courage and determination, we can reach the stars. We can find the peace and serenity we crave, and we can bask in the warm embrace of love and compassion if we let both into our lives.

Yes, I had a difficult journey because of a seemingly random event more than twenty-five years ago. If I'd given up, if I'd failed to try to make as much progress as I could in my recovery, my life would not be as rich and fulfilled as it is now. It just goes to show you that even when the hour looks to be the darkest, there is always the glimmer of dawn to look forward to. There's always change … inevitable change. The choice of how to respond to the changes that come to us all is up to each of us as individuals. What I learned from my experiences is that we are indeed the masters of our destinies, if we accept life as it comes and we live as truthfully and as purposefully as possible. It's all up to us. And we can do it! We just have to want to.

CPSIA information can be obtained
at www.ICGtesting.com
Printed in the USA
LVHW050005010721
691578LV00012B/1570

9 781532 095115